'This is a radical, enlivening cherry-bomb of a book. It brings something completely new to the current glut of publications about contemporary China. Steinfeld has spoken to hundreds of young, ambitious, hungry, confused, rebellious Chinese girls and boys, breaking taboos, getting personal *and* political. In doing so she reflects China as it really is, from the inside out, free of foreigners' speculation and rooted in the dynamic and contradictory social, economic and personal forces which are driving the hungriest and most rapidly transforming society in the world. This is a must-read for everyone from Sinophiles to sexophiles.'

Bidisha, journalist and broadcaster

'Jemimah Steinfeld's fresh and original book is outstanding. It shows us the hidden corners of Chinese society, where today's young Chinese are fighting for independence – torn between tradition and a fast-changing society, and confused by what they should want and who they should be.'

Xinran, author of *The Good Women of China*

'China's new generation will shape the global future. With insight and empathy, Jemimah Steinfeld portrays a generation caught between worlds, but striving to make their own.'

James Palmer, journalist at the *Global Times* and author of *The Death of Mao*

D0988460

LITTLE EMPERORS AND MATERIAL GIRLS

Sex and Youth in Modern China

JEMIMAH STEINFELD

I.B. TAURIS

LONDON · NEW YORK

Published in 2015 by
I.B.Tauris & Co. Ltd
London • New York
www.ibtauris.com

ISBN: 978 1 78076 984 4
eISBN: 978 0 85773 662 8

A full CIP record for this book is available from the British Library
A full CIP record is available from the Library of Congress

Typeset in Palatino by JCS Publishing Services Ltd,
www.jcs-publishing.co.uk

Printed and bound in Great Britain by T.J. International,
Padstow, Cornwall

MIX
Paper from
responsible sources
FSC® C013056

For the women of China,
who continue to triumph despite the obstacles.
May you soon hold up half the sky.

Contents

Acknowledgements

I would first like to thank everyone I interviewed and all those who make up the voices in this book. They were all incredibly kind in giving me their time and attention and, in most cases, opening up to a complete stranger. Without them *Little Emperors and Material Girls* would not exist.

In the same vein I would like to thank the team at I.B.Tauris and specifically my editor, Tomasz Hoskins. He saw a book in me before I did and his continued enthusiasm and support have been invaluable.

Special thanks go to my friend, teacher and translator Jean. Her kindness and patience knows no bounds.

Then there is my family. They've all encouraged me in their own way, both in writing the book and in exploring my continued fascination with China. My mother has been especially generous with her time and her editorial judgement.

Finally, there are my friends from inside and outside China. They've listened and given advice in equal measure. Particular mentions go to my housemate Laura, who allowed me to turn our living room into a writing enclave, and my partner, Simon, who helped me in the later stages.

Introduction
The Chinese Dream

The world is yours, as well as ours, but in the last
analysis, it is yours. You young people, full of vigour
and vitality, are in the bloom of life, like the sun at
eight or nine in the morning. Our hope is placed on
you. [...] The world belongs to you. China's future
belongs to you.
Chairman Mao (1957)

During the summer of 2013, millions of people throughout
China filed into their local cinemas to watch Chinese
chick flick *Tiny Times*. It was planned perfectly to coincide
with school and university holidays and the crowd was
predominantly young, lively and female. Hailed as China's
version of *Gossip Girl* and *Sex and the City*, *Tiny Times* had
taken the nation by storm. Immediately after its release, it set
a new box-office record and quickly knocked aside American
blockbuster *Man of Steel*. It became the most talked-about film
of the summer, turning it into a cultural – and multimillion-
dollar – phenomenon.

Based on a trio of popular young adult novels by Guo
Jingming, a 30-year-old celebrity author, *Tiny Times* narrates
the fortunes of four fashion-conscious Shanghai graduates
and their struggle for success, love and friendship. The movie
revolves around Lin Xiao, who lands her dream job as a personal
assistant at *ME*, a luxury fashion magazine. The publication's
title is no coincidence: the film is really a story about China's
'me' generation. These are the 1980s kids, the only children
born after China's reform and opening up, who care less about

politics and collectivism and more about individualism and conspicuous consumption.

Throughout the film, the characters trot around Shanghai in Christian Louboutins, drinking champagne like water. Outfit changes are frequent. No character appears wearing the same clothes twice, which, according to the production designer, resulted in more than 3,000 costumes. It's opulence on acid. 'Love without materialism is just a pile of sand,' proclaims one of the girls in the film as she admonishes her wealthy yet anti-consumerist onscreen boyfriend. In this world of commodities, a man is the ultimate accessory. The men in the film, as airbrushed as the women, are coveted and spoiled throughout. Their characters are reduced to little emperors, adored by the equally reductive material girls.

Does *Tiny Times* symbolise the Chinese dream?

Chinese commentators were divided. Critics of the film wrote about how the display of riches was gratuitous and the plots vacuous, in what quickly turned into a war of words over the morality of a new generation of young people. One esteemed film critic, Raymond Zhou, wrote that the film exhibited signs of 'pathological greed'. Another lamented the 'sick' parody of beauty and wealth. Were the youth of China becoming too materialistic?

In a related criticism, commentators wrote that if this was the Chinese dream, many would be disappointed. Most of the viewers were teenage girls hailing from one of China's second- or third-tier cities. Watching a film about China's super-rich was setting them up for consumerist expectations that could not be fulfilled. Their comments indicated that the gap between fiction and reality was not so entrenched in China as in the West, where we are used to films often exhibiting impossible lifestyles. For a Chinese teenager, whose parents could still remember collectivisation, and whose cinema historically conveyed messages from the Communist Party, the situation was different. This, then, was the heart of the issue. The China of the twenty-first century was nothing like the China of the twentieth – a fundamental difference between them and us.

While the West continues to change, it does so at a slower pace. It's a gentle gradient rather than a steep slope and therefore the schism between old and young is much less pronounced. Chinese commentators, an older bunch, were grappling with the direction China was taking and *Tiny Times* was a packaged version of their fears.

There was, in fact, some surprise that *Tiny Times* had been allowed to air at all. It was the first summer of the new Chinese politburo, with Xi Jinping as head of state. As the economy slowed for the first time in 14 years and the population grumbled about one too many corruption scandals, the Chinese government was on a campaign to promote austerity. It was not beyond the government to censor films that did not fit into their narrative, and *Tiny Times* was definitely walking a thin line. Eyebrows were raised about exactly where the central characters in the film got their money from. Those in intellectual circles were particularly fast to pick up on this.

But to China's youth, the popular appeal of *Tiny Times* was clear. It was a film about friendship, something which took on great meaning in a country where many of the under-thirties have no siblings. And it was about youth and hope. The rags-to-riches tale was seductive. This was buttressed by the film's writer and director, whose own story was proof that it wasn't all fantasy. Guo Jingming was born into a modest background in a small city in Sichuan Province in 1983. While at high school, he won first prize in a national writing competition for two consecutive years, which marked the beginning of his ascent towards fame. He then moved to Shanghai to study film, art and technology at university, a move he made on his own and with no help from his parents. He achieved overnight success when his book, *City of Fantasy* (2003), sold over 1.5 million copies and came second on the bestselling list in the first year of publication. Since then his star has continued to rise. He now runs a publishing empire, is one of the richest writers in China and is a regular fixture of the fashion circuit.

'For young readers, I am like a spokesman close to their age and experience, and so they connect with my work,' Guo once remarked. 'I used to be an ordinary student and my life resembles theirs in my writings: I studied, I was confused by the university entrance exam and I sometimes dated. Now I have become a tough person, so they aspire to who I am, which is also what they aspire towards in the world.'

Chen Shi-Zheng, an opera and film director, called Guo Jingming 'a brand for Chinese youth' and believed the controversy over *Tiny Times* stemmed from the comparative newness of youth culture.

And so, as millions continued to frequent the cinemas to see the movie, which was the first part of a very successful trilogy, fans hit back at the critics. They were labelled stick-in-the-muds who were out of touch with the young generation. 'You are insulting our young people. We have enthusiasm and dreams. We can fight for what we want,' wrote one person on Weibo, China's version of Twitter.

For many it was a much-needed bit of light entertainment during their summer holidays. 'It's fantastic and fun,' one 17-year-old told me when I posted asking whether it was worth watching. That girl was typing from a second-tier city in China's hinterland, Nanchong, in Sichuan Province. She told me her life was overwhelmingly defined by her studies. At the age of 16 her parents had sent her to boarding school in Chengdu, the capital city of Sichuan, in order for her to excel in the college entrance exam. Term times were hard and the cinema was off the agenda. The summer holidays were a moment of indulgence for her and four of her female friends, delighted with a night off at the movies. 'It's just drama, a way of escape. I live in the real world. It's impossible for common people to live this life,' she responded when asked if she aspired towards the lifestyle laid out in *Tiny Times*.

The amount of sex on display was also interesting – it was non-existent, which sat well with a nation still veering towards conservatism. Western critics were quick to highlight this omission, mocking it as *Sex and the City* without the sex. They missed the point. Not only would too much flesh have risked the heavy hand of censorship, it would have risked alienating the target audience. For plenty of Chinese viewers, the high sex content of shows in the West are literally and figuratively a turn-off. It is for this reason that the relatively tame Korean TV dramas do so well in China. The Confucian ideals of family and loyalty that these shows promulgate chime with Chinese ideals, which are also still heavily influenced by Confucianism and traditional values. To many, South Korea is seen as a model for modernisation. It remains highly conservative, suggesting that traditional values and modernity are not mutually exclusive.

Love it or loathe it, the film hit a nerve, and for that it could not be dismissed as merely cinematic candy floss. As China bulldozes its way to modernity at breakneck speed, the nation continues to ask: Who are we and where are we heading?

I too wanted to know the answers. In fact, these questions had kept me enthralled by China for the better part of a decade. I first came to the country in 2006. Like the characters in *Tiny Times*, I arrived in Shanghai and was instantly in awe, intoxicated by the pace and scale of life there. The cityscape changed on a daily basis, as new restaurants, bars and clubs opened. The city was abuzz and everyone I met was doing something beyond their nine-to-five jobs. But, as rickshaw drivers battled for space with new shiny Mercedes, asking who was benefiting from China's rise became unavoidable.

Since 2006 I have lived in China for two periods. During those times and upon my returns to London, this question has continued to bother me. The truth is that, whether you are in London, New York or anywhere else, the question of where the Chinese nation is heading is important. China is transfixing – and transforming – the world. And its youth are at the centre. They have always been the group who are the driving force of modern China. Chairman Mao himself was aware of this, throughout his life holding on to the notion that the future belonged to them. In a famous speech he made in 1957 to crowds of Chinese students and trainees in Moscow, he made the declaration which I quote at the top of this introduction.

For outsiders the question of Chinese youth and the future often concentrates on that of democracy and free speech. Could there be a repeat of Tiananmen Square, when thousands of students took to the streets of Beijing to ask for more political transparency? Or are the youth of today too transfixed by the famous motto 'To get rich is glorious', which started to circulate in the 1980s? Would a better standard of living make them search for greater freedoms or is their government giving them just enough of what they need? A lot of time is spent discussing whether Western-style democracy will come to China, but we should be unconvinced by the premise that China can be packaged so neatly into people who want wealth and are happy to give up their rights in return, and people who want democracy – as if the two are mutually exclusive. In a nation of 1.4 billion, with 300 million of those being under 30 – the size of the population of the United States – there are millions with a variety of modern interests, ambitions and aspirations.

As with all countries, China contains a spectrum of people from the politically apathetic to the politically engaged. This book is about the people we rarely read or hear about: the young people who are the first to feel the impact of some of the enormous wealth their country is generating, who are exposed to Western TV, movies and music, who have started to travel both within and outside their country. These people are also the generation raised by parents who lived through the Cultural Revolution and even have grandparents who remember a time when women had bound feet. They are being tugged in different directions, by tradition as much as by modernity. It's an oft-cited phrase that China is a country of contrasts and contradictions, but it is true. And the young are the people who feel it the most.

To this group, relationships are often the most important thing in their lives, and how they conduct their relationships reveals a lot about modern China. Whether it is fitting in with the pervasive attitude which places a premium on traditional roles, or rebelling against this, the youth of China are leading interesting love lives and sex lives, and their sexual attitudes and behaviour act as microcosms which show societal changes at large. It would be difficult to look at the youth of China without looking at changes in attitudes towards sex, love and the relationships between China's men and women.

So what of the sex and youth of today? As this book will show, the stories are as varied as China's many provinces. This does not mean trends do not emerge; they do. The trends just aren't always easily packaged. It's important to avoid falling into the trap of assuming that the sexual and youth revolutions going on inside China are mirroring those that have occurred in the West over the past 50 years. On the surface the changes that youth are experiencing seem to be much like a nascent form of ours. It may seem that people are becoming more promiscuous and more open to Western forms of entertainment; but if you dig beneath the surface you quickly see how wrong that assumption is and just how important it is to not predicate China's present and future on an extrapolation of our past. We in the West can find it difficult to imagine a trajectory that is not our own; we are imprisoned by an assumption that says progress will follow a Western model. Yet China's history and culture is unique and is shaping the country in its own ways. Ultimately change comes with Chinese characteristics.

Within the book are anecdotes from both ordinary and extraordinary Chinese people. I sought out those who could be labelled representative of a trend, whether they were leading the pack or following. I pried as much as I could and I always asked every one of them my two central questions: Are you married and, if not, do you want to be? From there a collection of varied stories unfolded.

As for the definition of youth, I don't want to home in on age as a number per se. Instead I see youth as more of a mindset. It's the transition period between becoming independent of parents and in turn becoming a parent, from being a late teenager to pre-marriage.

People interviewed for the book were largely those who had the resources to participate in new cultural activities. To some extent this cuts along financial lines, as money can be a prerequisite for access to new fashions and trends. It cut along educational lines to an extent too, as the ability to understand

and appreciate new ideas and movements was aligned to academia. Of course, people don't need wealth and a good education to participate in aspects of sex and youth culture. However, I wanted to talk to those whom I knew were central rather than peripheral, or those who were at least aware of changes and were making an active decision to lead their lives in one way or another, as opposed to following a more passive line from lack of choice. These are China's new middle classes. Determining these people as the voices of their generation – those who potentially hold the key to the country's future – I wanted to know and chronicle more on what they did, what they thought and what they had to say.

Finally, the book is set mostly in Beijing, though accounts from elsewhere are brought in as and when they are complementary. This is because so much change takes place in China's capital. While Shanghai (and to a lesser extent Guangzhou) might be the financial heart of the mainland, Beijing is still the political and cultural nucleus. The metropolis is a melting pot of different forces: old meets new; reactionary meets reformist; local meets national meets international. All of these pulls are inescapable in Beijing. There is nothing airbrushed about the city. It's raw and guttural. It's China.

The book has been divided into three sections: Love and Dating; Sex and Sexuality; China's Now Generation. Within this structure we can see a snapshot of modern Chinese youth and the issues and trends shaping them. The title of *Little Emperors and Material Girls* has been chosen for a reason. These labels, used by the Chinese themselves, are social constructs not realities and it is the interplay between the sexes and between rhetoric and reality that makes twenty-first-century China such a fascinating place.

LOVE AND DATING

1

Leftover in Beijing

*Entire dinners are spent discussing my love life.
It's ridiculous!*
Wei Na, on being single above the age of 27

It is another severely polluted day in Beijing when I meet Wei Na. The tops of buildings are barely visible and the streets are full of people wearing face masks. Some don ones that can easily be picked up from convenience stores, flimsy pale blue numbers that resemble surgical masks. Others wear the expensive kind; large, black and replete with air vents. They look like Darth Vaders. Most simply resign themselves to the situation and leave the house without any armour, going about their day-to-day tasks against a backdrop of thick, stagnant smog. Try as they might to ignore it, though, air pollution is all anyone can talk about. Like the British and the weather, Beijingers are obsessed with air quality.

Wei Na is running late. When she arrives she looks flustered, her black fringe pushed to the side by a gel of sweat, and a pink hue gives colour and contour to her otherwise white, angular face. 'The traffic is terrible today,' she complains, in clear punctuated English. '*Mei wenti*,' I reply. 'No problem.' I joke about whether the traffic is ever good, memories flooding back of being in one of the longest recorded jams in history in central Beijing. 'Today is "crazy bad",' I add, in reference to the US Embassy's gaff about air quality. The Embassy – much to the chagrin of the Chinese government – has been documenting levels of air pollution on Twitter for years. On one occasion, when the levels rose especially high, the feed broke and simply read 'crazy bad'. Apparently the technician behind it never thought the meter would go above a certain recording and added the code 'crazy bad' as a joke if it did. They were wrong. The joke remains: a testament to the fact that even in grim conditions the inhabitants of Beijing have a sense of humour.

Wei Na sits down and scans the menu. We are in a restaurant in Beijing's modern, affluent neighbourhood, Sanlitun. A mixture of trendy locals and expats fill the place, tucking into gourmet salads and sandwiches that promise to be made using only the freshest ingredients. You pay Western prices for this privilege, but many young Beijingers feel it is worth it to know you are eating food that won't be headline news under the title 'food scandal'. Recently glow-in-the-dark pork has been exposed, joining a long list of food contaminated by various chemicals which still manage to make their way to the market.

Like the food, the restaurant surroundings are surgically clean and orderly. It is in sharp contrast to the mayhem outside. In fact, the whole experience feels like a vacuum, a protective shield from all the pollutants elsewhere. The service is polite and attentive. The *fuwuyuan* – waiter – soon appears and takes our order. Wei Na lets out a deep sigh.

'I've just spent the morning fighting with my aunt,' she says. 'She doesn't approve of my boyfriend.'

Wei Na lives with her aunt and uncle on the outskirts of Beijing. She has been there for ten years. Her parents live in Qinghai, a province in China's north-west, near Tibet, and she moved to Beijing at the age of 18 when she accepted a place at a top university in the capital.

Getting into one of Beijing's universities, some of which are the equivalent of Harvard and Yale in China, as a non-Beijing resident sets Wei Na in an exclusive class. The *gaokao* – the two-day college entrance exams – are notoriously hard, so much so that they have been linked to spikes in teenage suicide. At the same time, cut-off scores to get into Chinese universities vary for *gaokao* test-takers from different provinces, based on population size and other variables. They are lower for remote provinces such as Hainan and Tibet, ensuring a form of affirmative action to students with relatively little educational resources. Conversely, the cut-off scores are also inexplicably low in Beijing and Shanghai, two municipalities with the best educational resources in the country. Qinghai, a large province with a small population and an equally small economy, would have benefited from lower scores. But it was still no mean feat and Wei Na had to work very hard at school to secure a top place.

Fresh out of college with a degree in business and excellent English skills, Wei Na gained employment at a high-end cashmere company working in their exports department. She has risen through the ranks and regularly travels to Europe. Wei Na's story is exemplary for these reasons. She is a rare breed in Beijing, one of the city's high-flyers, and yet she shares many of the concerns of other people her age.

Wei Na lived in college dorms throughout her time at university. There several people shared basic rooms with bunk beds. Communal showers were at the other end of campus, which was a particular inconvenience during the winter. Once out of university, she decided to move in with her aunt and uncle, who lived in an apartment located in one of Beijing's emerging well-heeled suburbs.

Her decision to move in with the family was in part financially motivated. The cost of housing in Beijing, and in all of urban China, is soaring. When I first came to the country, back in 2006, it was possible to rent a room in a high-end property in central Shanghai, the most expensive city in mainland China, for little more than the equivalent of £300 a month. By 2013 that was at the lower end. 'Shanghai New Home Prices up 273 Percent in 7 Years', read one headline. In fact, prices jump significantly from month to month, let alone year to year. In February 2013, Beijing property prices were 3.1 per cent higher than the previous month. According to a 2013 report published around the same time, this is an 82 per cent increase on what they were in 2008, with experts believing the key cause to be a serious imbalance between supply and demand in the housing sector. Landlords are cashing in; 40 per cent increases in rent from the previous year are not uncommon.

Government efforts to cool the property market in 2014 have been largely ineffectual. Housing remains unaffordable for most, including high-earners, and public opinion polls continue to rank rising home prices as one of the biggest sources of anxiety for Chinese adults.

The imbalance seems hard to believe when you visit a modern Chinese city; construction of a major housing project happens everywhere, at all hours of the day. In Beijing the urban facelift appears particularly pronounced. Only a century ago, the city was low-rise, made up almost entirely of one-storey complexes. Regulations forbade residents building anything higher than the emperor's throne. With the toppling of the imperial regime, these restrictions were lifted. Now the old residences look feeble as new-builds tower over them, ready to swallow them up at any given second. It's a familiar sight in modern Chinese cities, most of which have taken on similar, soulless characteristics.

As fast as new complexes go up, people are moving faster still. It's a trend that is likely to continue. At the start of 2012, the Chinese government announced that China was predominantly urban for the first time in its long history. City dwellers represented just 10.6 per cent of the population in 1949 and just under 19 per cent in 1979, when the market reforms were launched. Now they're over 50 per cent and rising. It is predicted that by 2020 China's burgeoning cities will be home to 800 million people, up from 666 million in 2010. Those who can live rent-free with relatives and avoid the housing circus often do so in China, to the point of marriage, and sometimes beyond.

It is not just financial concerns that influence Wei Na's decision to live with her relatives. In China, the family is still paramount. One of the few consistent ideas to have survived the recent decades of chaos is that of filial piety, the principle of respecting your parents and ancestors. For centuries filial piety has been articulated through citation of Confucian philosophy, which, despite the Communist government attacking it as 'feudal', has never quite gone out of fashion. And where Confucian philosophy stops, aphorisms start. 'Filial piety is the root of all virtues,' goes one popular saying.

The concept is particularly important for girls. A pamphlet of a 1935 Confucian nationalist organisation read: 'Women are born with filial feminine and ethical debt. So the purpose of their lives is to clear that debt.' Times have obviously changed since this pamphlet was penned, both in terms of female liberation and the liberation of children from endless duties to their parents, as reflected by their domesticities alone: whereas once several generations shared the same dwelling, living in intimate neighbourhoods and courtyard houses, by 2011 more than half of all Chinese over the age of 60 lived separately from their grown children, according to statistics from China's National Committee on Ageing.

Of course this still means nearly half of the over-sixties live with their children. It seems to be a very close structure when you come from a culture where kids move out of home upon going to college and grandparents live away from parents. Closeness isn't necessarily bad; the Chinese reverence for the aged is refreshing and it's always a pleasure to see the elderly out and about on the streets instead of hidden away in old people's homes, as we have grown accustomed to in Western societies. The Western model, if anything, is feared by the Chinese; as fewer Chinese live with their families and retirement homes start to appear across the nation, a sense that the younger generation is neglecting ageing parents has emerged. It's a well-articulated fear: in a country where the generation gap is larger than in most and where the population is ageing, what the older generation wants still matters. Hence the passage of the Elderly Rights Law, which came into effect in July 2013. This law allows older people to sue their children for neglect and acts as a both real and symbolic reminder of the importance of filial piety.

Filial piety is not a huge burden for Wei Na. She has a good relationship with her aunt and uncle and can largely get on with her life with minimal interference. Mostly they are very supportive. Like many young people in the city, Wei Na's primary concern has been to establish a good career. Having lived through the infamous Great Leap Forward of 1958–61, which resulted in a famine killing tens of millions, her aunt and uncle are aware of hardship and appreciate the value of financial security. Like millions of others, they remember a time when China was a developing country and can unite on an ethos of hard work.

However, some of her lifestyle choices are lost on them. Specifically, until recently, establishing a relationship has been a secondary concern for Wei Na, an attitude very much at odds with her aunt and uncle, who are still hardwired to think that marriage is the ultimate goal of a woman. As she has grown older, the pressure from her family has mounted.

'Entire dinners are spent discussing my love life. It's ridiculous! We will sit down and all eyes will be on me for the next two hours,' she says, explaining how she avoids going home until late, working overtime or meeting up with friends.

Then, at the age of 29, after many years of pressure from her family about her single status, she met Yeping. Yeping is 30 and a tattoo artist. Their paths crossed at the gym; she already had a tattoo below her belly button and decided to get another. As she says this, I scan her bare arms and legs. Noticing my curiosity, she lifts up her top to reveal a snake wrapped around her midriff. This exposure gives me a hint of why her aunt might not approve of her boyfriend. Although every Chinese child is taught the legend of Yue Fei, a twelfth-century general whose mother tattooed 'serve the country with utmost loyalty' on his back, tattoos have a bad reputation in China, having long been associated with criminals and organised gangs. During the Cultural Revolution of the 1960s and 1970s, Chairman Mao Zedong actually banned tattoos, calling them a manifestation of impurity and roguery. Even today, military personnel, for example, are not allowed them. Similarly, some enterprises have a policy of not hiring people with tattoos or other body ornaments.

China's youth are less concerned by these attitudes and have adopted tattoos as part of their fashion, challenging long-held prejudices. Not everyone has updated their views. Many of the older generation in particular still oppose the idea of covering the body with visible and sometimes provocative art. When Wei Na's father spotted her tattoo, he literally rouged with rage.

'Only criminals have tattoos!' he yelled. Her new boyfriend is therefore a criminal in his eyes.

'It's not like in the West where the individual and their love life has nothing to do with their family. Mine have to be made happy,' she adds.

Wei Na is in a lose–lose situation: doomed if she breaks up with Yeping and doomed if she stays with him. She is what the Chinese label a *'sheng nu'*, a leftover woman – a term used to describe any single woman over the age of 27. The term was officially endorsed by the Chinese government in 2007 when the Women's Federation stipulated its exact definition and China's Ministry of Education subsequently added it to its official lexicon. In its narrowest sense, it simply translates as single women of a certain age, but its colloquial use also denotes women who are well-educated, affluent urban dwellers, whose standards are deemed very (too) high.

Sheng nu are derided within China. Take this excerpt from a column that was published just days after International Women's Day in March 2011 on the Women's Federation website:

Pretty girls don't need a lot of education to marry into a rich and powerful family, but girls with an average or ugly appearance will find it difficult. These kinds of girls hope to further their education in order to increase their competitiveness. The tragedy is, they don't realise that as women age, they are worth less and less, so by the time they get their MA or PhD, they are already old, like yellowed pearls.

It continues:

Many highly educated 'leftover women' are very progressive in their thinking and enjoy going to nightclubs to search for a one-night stand, or they become the mistress of a high official or rich man. It is only when they have lost their youth and are kicked out by the man, that they decide to look for a life partner. Therefore, most leftover women do not deserve our sympathy.

The message is not subtle. Women's self-betterment comes from marriage, not education. Rather than heralding 'progressiveness', the Federation see it as an enemy, presenting arguments that haven't been heard in the West for decades. To be sure, there are gender battles of a different nature still to be fought and won in the West, but those who lament the entrance of women into the workforce are marginalised. Not so in China. The Women's Federation, founded in 1949 to protect women's rights and interests, sits at the centre of conversations on gender. A significant part of Mao's manifesto when he came to power was that 'women hold up half the sky' and the Women's Federation was put in charge of making this a reality. Whilst the Federation has achieved a lot, such as raising literacy levels amongst women and campaigning to raise awareness and helping tackle child and female trafficking, it is still reactionary on social issues.

Its publication of negative articles about single women has been a constant. A quick tour of its website is a lesson in anger management. 'Overcoming the Big Four Emotional Blocks: Leftover Women Can Break Out of Being Single', 'Eight Simple Moves to Escape the Leftover Women Trap' and 'Do Leftover Women Really Deserve our Sympathy?' are just a few of the headlines.

At one stage the Women's Federation added sub-genres. In 'See What Category of Leftover You Belong To' it assigned young, single women to slots according to their age. 'Leftover Fighters' are those aged between 25 and 27, 'The ones who must triumph' are between 28 and 30 and 'Master class of leftover women' are the over-35s.

Why is this supposed champion of Chinese female liberation leading a campaign to make women less independent? One reason is the resurgence in traditional gender roles;

the Women's Federation is simply channelling beliefs held by the population at large. Another persuasive theory in circulation is that of demography. According to Leta Hong Fincher, author of *Leftover Women: The Resurgence of Gender Inequality in China*, the Women's Federation has got into bed with the government. In 2007, just when the term *sheng nu* came into parlance, China's State Council issued an edict on strengthening the Population and Family Planning programme to address 'unprecedented population pressures'. These pressures include the sex ratio imbalance – which 'causes a threat to social stability' – and the 'low quality of the general population, which makes it hard to meet the requirements of fierce competition for national strength'. The State Council names 'upgrading population quality' as a primary goal and has appointed the Women's Federation as the main implementer of its population planning policy.

Fincher's observations make a great deal of sense. China is facing a demographic time bomb, with a huge ageing population and a diminishing workforce. At the same time, there are more boys than girls in China. China's long-standing preference for boys, exacerbated by the One Child Policy introduced in 1978, has led to a ratio of 100 girls to every 118 boys. National Bureau of Statistics data estimate there are currently 20 million more men under 30 than women under 30. By 2020 the number of excess men is predicted to match the population of Texas. If single women do not settle down, these numbers will become greater.

The increasing pool of single men has its own social definition: '*guang gun*', a bare branch. In other words, a man who will not add to the family tree if he remains single. The *guang gun* are mostly a rural phenomenon. Of the estimated 40 to 50 million bare branches scattered across China, most of them are concentrated in rural and poorer areas. There are, it is said, entire villages without any single women in them. This is because Chinese men generally marry down in terms of education and age. There is a prevailing opinion that 'alpha' men will go for 'beta' women, leaving the alpha women and beta men with fewer options. Alpha women are usually in the cities; beta men in the countryside.

It is a vicious cycle. Bare branches do not have the money to make it to a city, and without money and unable to live in an urban, more populated space, their chances of meeting and attracting single women are much lower. Thus while census figures for China show that around one in five women aged 25–29 are unmarried and the proportion of unmarried men that age is over a third higher, the two groups do not often come into contact.

'I WOULD RATHER CRY IN A BMW': CLICHÉD VIEWS OF WHAT CHINESE WOMEN WANT

There is a hidden irony behind China's continued preference for boys. For the first time in its long history, it is turning women into hot commodities. It is an unintended inversion of centuries of patriarchal rule. Girls below a certain age can now wield a degree of power when it comes to choosing a spouse.

So what do these demographically empowered women want? A cliché runs that Chinese girls expect future husbands to be rich and successful. The cliché has been propagated by women just as much as men. For example, on a very popular dating show in 2010, *Fei Cheng Wu Rao* (*If You Are the One*), 20-year-old contestant Ma Nuo vocalised what many Chinese girls are believed to be thinking when she famously declared that she would 'rather cry in a BMW than laugh on the backseat of a bicycle'.

Ma's comment closely coincided with a woman called Long Siyu, then 23, and 15 of her friends posting an online video on Youku, China's answer to YouTube, chastising men for not owning their own house or car.

'If you don't have a car and you don't have a house, please move aside, don't block my way,' chimed one girl in the clip. The video was an overnight sensation. Within 48 hours of it being uploaded, the song had been viewed 1.5 million times.

It is not just on the airwaves that girls demand affluence in a man. Gong Haiyan, the female founder of China's biggest dating website, Jiayuan, says that the key attributes women are searching for online are a man's height, salary and whether or not he owns a house and a car. In Beijing only 12 per cent of men using the site own their own home, which means most of the women on the website are fighting over this 12 per cent.

Have Chinese women become shallow? The story is complicated. Firstly, the BMW comment is believed to have been fabricated. In order to attract high ratings, Ma was fed that line by the production team. It has since been swallowed whole by many as evidence that China is full of material girls. It's a weapon; the cascade of claims in the media that women are too picky couple nicely with stories of leftover women to play on Chinese women's insecurities. Even if some women do want a wealthy husband (and this is by no means an exclusively Chinese phenomenon), Chinese women are facing other setbacks when it comes to equal opportunities – as will be explored in further detail later in the book – and these setbacks are feeding their desire to marry up out of a sense of pragmatism.

In reality what Chinese women want cannot be packaged into one box. Some young women talk of wealthy partners, some of humour, compassion and other characteristics. Either way, it seems that few are winners in the Chinese dating world. The consequence of rural females marrying up and out is men in the countryside left wifeless and lonely. At the same time, women in the cities, who are meant to have more options, find themselves feeling guilty, lacking and desperately trying to avoid pressures, both economic and familial.

BARE BRANCHES AND EATING BITTERNESS: THE ONE CHILD POLICY

Yeping has spent all of his life in Beijing. As a child he grew up in a house in a *hutong*, the name given to Beijing's old lanes. The house had no central heating and no indoor bathroom or toilet. Yeping had to walk a few minutes down the road to get to the communal facilities. Then, as China became richer and its cityscapes started to transform, Yeping's parents decided to move to a modern block a few miles away from where he grew up. The decision was all theirs; it was not the result of forced relocation, though there are plenty of people in Beijing who have been forced to move as the city modernises.

As was the fate of many of Beijing's old lanes, Yeping's *hutong* no longer exists. In the past few decades, despite the government's commitment on paper to heritage conservation, two-thirds of Beijing's 3,000 *hutong* – some of which have formed the capital's core since the thirteenth century – have been torn down as heritage protection has lost out to development. UNESCO estimates that 88 per cent of the city's courtyard homes have been destroyed in the process.

There are many people in Beijing who lament the destruction of the lanes. China's foreign community for one, since these higgledy-piggledy streets with their curved-roof houses feed into fantasies of old-world charm. Then there are the local Beijingers whose childhood memories are attached to these areas and who refuse to accept that the new high-rise architecture represents 'real' Beijing. The 2013 opening of the Shijia Hutong Museum – which attempts to preserve their memory – shows just how far the attachment to these lanes goes.

However, not all mourn the *hutong*. Most were considered unsanitary and incompatible with the modern age. The new builds might be charmless, but at least they are functional. Tom Miller perfectly summarises the friction felt over the *hutong* in his book *China's Urban Billion*. In response to allegations that they are slums, he writes:

> Beijing's villages are neither the tuberculosis-ridden rookeries of Dickens' London nor the cholera-filled shanty towns of modern Mumbai. They are neither sordid nor disease-ridden. But they are overcrowded and shoddily constructed; they enjoy few public services and amenities; and the narrow, rubbish-strewn streets and alleyways quickly flood

when the summer rains arrive. Rooms are typically poky and cold, with low ceilings and little natural light. Villagers share communal outdoor lavatories – iceboxes in winter – squatting side by side in un-partitioned rows of three.

The Beijing Yeping grew up in was therefore markedly different to today's city. Of particular resonance for him, there were few tattoo parlours when he was younger, so he used himself and his friends as canvases for practice. Then, aged 18, he got an apprenticeship. There was little demand for tattoos when he started out, and Yeping lived on very little, commuting across town by bus for two hours, only to arrive at a dark, dilapidated room in the basement of a market. With no regulation from the state, needles would be reused.

As demand for tattoos increased, so did the supply of tattoo parlours. There are now hundreds in Beijing, and Yeping has been able to work his way up the ladder. When I meet him he is managing a parlour located on the ground floor of a gargantuan shopping mall frequented by Beijing's young, hipster crowd who have taken to Western forms of art and style.

Yeping was born in 1981, three years after the One Child Policy was instituted. While circumventing the policy has been possible for those living in the countryside, those in the city are more closely watched and controlled, making it very difficult to have more offspring, unless parents have the funds to pay the excoriating fines the government imposes on violators. Yeping therefore grew up as an only child.

Even though neither Yeping nor his parents wished to fall out, they could not help feel distant from one another as their interests were at loggerheads. A disjuncture between parents and offspring is a common phenomenon in modern China. 'It's an extreme generation gap,' I was told one day by a 33-year-old who had spent some years studying in America. 'There's a gap in wealth, education, technology and information. Our values are different because our lives are so different,' explained the girl as she played with her new HTC smartphone. 'I love my parents, but we have very little in common. They try to be supportive, but ultimately they can't relate to the life I lead, and I would go crazy if I led the same life as them!'

Of course it is not unheard of for parents to be confused by their children in the West. There are plenty above a certain age who are only just getting to grips with predictive text as the younger generation surge ahead. However, in the West there is usually a degree of continuity between the different generations. Changes are in scale not kind. This is not the case in China. The parents of China's post-1980s generation grew up in a world completely different to the one their children occupy. Having choice alone is novel. In the predominantly rural Maoist world of the 1960s and 1970s, people's lives were dictated from above, as they were assigned where they could live, where they would work and when they would work. And, of course, most older people in China have siblings. Just 27 per cent of those born in 1975 are only children; in 1983, it rose to 91 per cent, though others place the number lower.

Because of these stark differences, a name has emerged for the post-Maoist generation – *balinghou*. Born after 1980, during China's reform and opening-up period, the *balinghou* are said not to know how to *chi ku*, or 'eat bitterness', because they have never experienced real hardship. They are believed to have certain psychological traits. In the words of one Hong Konger I met, who has three siblings: 'It's impossible to get close to a Mainlander. They don't understand intimacy and trust because they hardly experienced it at home as kids.'

This is a generalisation that is being made elsewhere. A lot of research has been conducted into what effect a whole nation of only children is producing, with the assumption being that it must be having some impact at a national level. The results have been mixed. In 1993, a study found that Chinese children did better academically and the personalities of only children were seen as no different from their peers with siblings. Since then some have concluded that Chinese children, who start school relatively young, use their schoolmates to make up for lack of playmates at home.

Other survey results – those quoted more in the Chinese media – are less flattering. According to a study published in 2013 in the academic journal *Science*, these kids are less competitive, less trusting, less altruistic, more risk averse and more neurotic than those with siblings.

THE RISE OF THE LITTLE EMPERORS

When it comes to considering the problems of China's only children, men are specifically singled out. With China's continued preference for boys, the worst offenders are considered to be boys. This has given rise to the term *xiao huangdi* – little emperor.

In his memoir *On the Move: An Immigrant Child's Global Journey*, computer scientist Philip Jia Guo, who was born in 1983 in Zhongshan, describes what his Chinese childhood was like:

> I had everything that I wanted. Due to the bias of traditional Chinese culture towards male children, my extended family treated me like a pampered Little Emperor since I was not only the first-born son of my generation, but I was also the only son of my generation throughout my early childhood. They all spoiled me with special attention and preferential treatment, and my parents were not around to teach me about restraint. I enjoyed the privilege of always having plenty of toys, fancy clothes, good food to eat, people to drive me to amusement parks, and relatives always catering to my endless demands.

Of course, anyone who has lived in China will have met plenty of successful and open only child men, but the perception still exists within China that these are little emperors. It has been reported that some employers specify 'no single children' in job postings. For parents with the means, hundreds of summer 'hardship' camps have sprung up throughout the country that seek to instil in children the values they are supposedly lacking. These can take the form of a boot camp at a military base, where children up to the age of 18 are stripped of all personal belongings upon arrival and made to undergo weeks of intense training. Or they can involve children camping in impoverished areas of the country as a form of shock therapy. There are even camps for parents to learn how to discipline their children. They all form part of an elaborate attempt to remove the supposed emperors from their thrones.

It is easy to take a dig at these kids, but there is something quite unenviable about their situation. A 2012 survey revealed that 58 per cent of respondents described how having no siblings left them feeling lonely and selfish. As Liu Yi, author of *I Am Not Happy: The Declaration of an '80s Generation Only Child*, explained: 'We are the unfortunate ones because we are only children. Fate destined us with less happiness than other children from other generations. We are also the lucky ones – with attention from so many adults, we skip over childish ignorance and grow up fast.'

The first generations of only children have now come of age and are becoming parents themselves. With this, fear for the next generation is rising. After all, the first generation at least had aunts and uncles – often many, as the generation before were encouraged to procreate under Mao. The next generation will not benefit from such a dynamic. Out of this fear has arisen the concept of 'child marriage', when parents actively find playmates for their children in the hope that they will act as surrogate siblings.

Talk of abolishing the One Child Policy altogether has also become more prevalent. In recent years the rules have been relaxed, first allowing partnerships involving two only children to have two children themselves and now allowing those where only one parent is an only child to have two children.

Turning back to Yeping, our bare branch, he confided that he felt lonely growing up. Both his parents worked hard and he was often home alone, sitting in front of the TV playing computer games. Wei Na was considered fortunate – she had an elder sister because she was delivered in Hong Kong – one way some families circumvent the policy. Yeping asked her what it was like to grow up with siblings. It was not the first time Wei Na had had this conversation.

I meet Yeping in person several weeks after I met Wei Na. It's a Friday night and Wei Na has arranged to come out with me and some friends. The agenda is dinner, followed by bar-hopping. The idea of going on to KTV – karaoke – has been suggested, which is usual for any night out in China. No matter how good or bad the voice, a communal sing-along is one of the most popular pastimes for young people, as is watching Chinese equivalents of *X Factor*. If nothing else, China is a nation of aspiring pop idols.

I arrive a few minutes early at the restaurant. Ten minutes later, Wei Na walks through the door. She is wearing a slinky white dress with holes cut in the sides. The snake peers out from one. She passes a table of Chinese men puffing away on cigarettes as though they are keeping the tobacco industry afloat. Smoking indoors has been banned for several years in China, yet no one seems to honour this. The men all turn their heads. Yeping is in tow, with one long, muscular arm draped possessively over Wei Na's shoulder. He is tall, with a kind face, and is wearing baggy skater trousers and a trucker hat. Save for his head, there is very little visible flesh on his body left unmarked or unpierced.

The sake is already flowing by the time they arrive and the atmosphere is warm and congenial. Yet it quickly becomes clear that Yeping does not want to talk. Instead he perches himself at the side of the group and starts to play on his phone. The Chinese at the table don't find the behaviour as odd as the foreigners do. Wei Na, Chinese herself, yet versed in Western table etiquette, shoots us a look that says sorry. As the food arrives, Yeping's gaze hardly shifts from his phone. Unsurprisingly, at the end of the meal, he makes his excuses and leaves.

Wei Na tells me later that it was not the first time he had acted in this way. Yeping's only interest is in Wei Na herself, not her friends. They are superfluous and irrelevant in his eyes. She has told him many times that her friends matter to her. He seems not to care.

'He rarely compromises with his parents and is used to getting his own way. He's such a typical little emperor!' Wei Na exclaims. She continues going out with him for a few more weeks before eventually ending the relationship. She decides she would rather be 29 and single than 29 and settling.

'My aunt was initially happy. Then she remembered my age and tried to have a serious talk with me about being *sheng nu*. I told her that more than ever before I wasn't going to rush into marrying anyone, that my happiness does not just come from having a boyfriend. I know she is still worried though,' Wei Na tells me several weeks after they broke up.

'You shouldn't settle,' I tell her by way of encouragement. She is an attractive, successful girl who is still ultimately very young. But I know my words will not ease her anxiety. I have had many conversations with Chinese girls about this very same topic – girls who are a mix of anxious and despondent about being single. The anxiety reaches its peak during national holidays. Wei Na has not seen her parents for about seven months, since the Chinese New Year break. In China, companies award very little personal holiday allowance. I recall when I was first told at the Chinese newspaper where I worked that my annual holiday allowance was five working days. I thought they were joking.

It is somewhat made up for by a generous portion of annual holidays: the country has approximately 18 days of statutory national holiday, with Chinese New Year and the National Holiday both being week-long events. As so many Chinese live and work far away from their native towns and villages and rarely get an opportunity to travel home, these treasured family get-togethers are weighted with pressure, much more so than Christmas and Thanksgiving in the West. Accomplishments must be displayed, and finding a significant other is top of the list. If you are not with someone, well-wishers will say they hope you bring someone back next time. The less kind will castigate you with a tut-tut, closely followed by a comment about other people who have found commitment. The pressure is particularly felt by Chinese women, as their career achievements are undervalued. Men face it too, though. China still emphasises the community above the individual; you are letting your community down if you do not wed.

The pressure has become so great that you can now hire boyfriends on Taobao, China's eBay equivalent. 'Not getting any younger and still dreading facing the nagging parents?' reads one advertisement circulating on Taobao, where for the equivalent of around £100 you can rent someone for a whole day. The nature of this is usually innocent – a direct response to mounting familial pressure. Some, though, advertise euphemistically labelled 'extras', which can be bought upon presentation of a health certificate.

My exchanges with Wei Na are typical of those I have with other Chinese youth. People in the West often ask what it's like to live in China's capital. Does it feel like a police state? Do I notice the censorship? Are the Chinese people angry that they do not have democracy? These people's views of China have been formed through the prism of the Western press, which tends towards hyperbolic articles, painting the country as an emotional and physical prison. Of course elements of this are true. However, what a visitor finds most striking is that the daily lives and interactions of urban middle-class Chinese are not so dissimilar from their own. People in their late twenties talk about clothes, books and shows on TV, they worry about their health, weight and work. And most of all they talk about and want to find love.

Yet, whilst their interests and concerns are not unlike our own, the scale is often more pronounced. What happens in China always feels like a magnification of events that are going on elsewhere. For example, there is corruption in the UK, but in China it is rife. London is polluted; Beijing is choking. This, after all, is the country that has given birth to entire towns devoted to the manufacture of the world's supplies of certain products, and where an unheard-of city can still easily be home to 10 million residents. When it comes to love, the same is true. In the West, parents have expectations; they want to see their offspring settled down with someone nice. And ideally they want to have grandchildren. However, in the West this burden is usually spread across several children and more understated. In China the pressure often rests on the shoulders of their one child and against the backdrop of a country with a significant gender bias and imbalance. Finding love is arguably more important than ever, but it is also becoming a battlefield reserved for the bravest.

It is heartening to know that Wei Na stood firm. Lots of women in her position might not have done. I know of some Chinese girls who are consciously settling, rushing into relationships and marriages with people they are unsure of. I have even met a woman who, terrorised by tales of *sheng nu*, quit her job because she thought she would find it easier to attract a husband. Others do not give up work entirely but are turning down promotions or opting for 'less ambitious' career paths. A former colleague once told me that she desperately wanted to be a doctor. Instead she entered media because her mother thought it would be a more fitting profession to attract a husband. 'The hours are less long and the pay will not scare a man off,' her mother had advised. 'Women are nurses not doctors,' was another phrase reported back to me. The girl consoles herself by writing health articles. Stories such as these are sad and demoralising. They fly in the face of the female liberation movement being about choice; women in China are still trapped by a patriarchal society which says they must perform certain roles. In short, it is a far cry from Mao's promise that women would hold up half the sky.

FINDING LOVE AT THE MARKET

In Beijing in September the weather is at its balmy best. For most of the year Beijing is held captive by the seasons. Winters are long, dry and freezing. Summers, while equally long, are boiling and accompanied by rainstorms. Spring and autumn are such short periods of reprieve, they almost feel like afterthoughts. It is during these two brief seasons that a calmness takes hold of the air. Your muscles relax and you can finally enjoy being outside. Even though this serenity is always laced with a sense of foreboding at the next approaching season, it is still the best time to be out and about in a city marked by its extreme weather.

I am walking in a typical Beijing park, hidden behind a high wall with grass and trees that look scorched and deprived of chlorophyll. Old grey-haired women gather around in a circle to do communal exercises next to men immersed in games of mah-jong.

Then, around a corner, a large, frenetic crowd of middle-aged people congregate, milling between rows of photographs of younger people. I have stumbled across one of China's love markets, where parents go to meet fellow parents of single children in the hope of orchestrating a match.

It is not the first time I have found myself in the middle of a love market. Youngsters' unwillingness to marry young has spurred anxiety amongst an older generation and these love markets are one result. They can be found in parks across China. When I lived in Shanghai, on Saturday mornings I would regularly walk through People's Square in the centre of the city, where parents would congregate for the same purpose. Back then it took a while to figure out what was going on. Sheets were hanging from trees like laundry in the wind and my first thought was of Chinese calligraphy.

A few people look me up and down, trying to figure out if I am 'shopping'. I approach some of the résumés, in order to get a better look. I am greeted by the usual silence that I have come to expect when a foreigner shows interest in something so obviously Chinese. Then they go back to the business at hand. In the Beijing love market they clearly have a lot to keep them occupied, exchanging details and phone numbers in the manner of a professional networking event.

The descriptions of their children are all quite similar and – surprisingly – most of them are sons. On tattered A4 sheets, key characteristics are homed in on: salary, age, height and education. One stands out in particular. It is a large framed photo of a boy at his graduation. It's a fairly standard shot, the one proud parents display on their mantelpiece. Only this one is not from a Chinese university. It is from Stanford.

'Your son is handsome and he must be very clever,' I tell the man holding the picture. He responds with a dumbfounded expression, before turning to the person next to him and whispering something inaudible about '*waiguoren*' – foreigners. I persist. What does his son think about his father acting as cupid? Finally, a response: 'He likes it. He works very hard, has little time to meet women. I help him!'

It's a little perplexing why someone with an edge in the love market needs their parents to help them find a date, but I've been in China for long enough to realise that there's a strong chance the son doesn't actually know his father is here; or if he does, he might occasionally go along with plans such as these to appease the parents. I'm soon elbowed out of the way by a pushy mother, clearly hoping to be an in-law to Mr Stanford. I continue my walk.

I half expect to see a picture of either Wei Na or Yeping here. I don't, which shouldn't come as a surprise. There are, after all, officially 20 million people living here and this figure does not include the migrant population, which could add another 10 million. Of these, around 500,000 are unmarried twenty-something women.

In many ways this is a story which sums up a lot of the themes outlined in this book. Wei Na and Yeping are typical of a new generation of Chinese youth. Their pressures are national pressures in modern China – an acutely felt generation and gender gap, familial pressure, conflicted aspirations, pressures to find love and explore their newfound sexual freedoms, and a sense of breathlessness in fast-evolving China.

2

Reality Bytes
The Emergence of the Internet in China

If you go to the pool, you need to learn to swim by yourself.
Shu, 27, an online dater

It's not easy for young Chinese people to meet each other. Many report feelings of loneliness and alienation. In a world where meeting other singles is difficult, and in a China which looks nothing like it did just a decade ago, the internet has become a lifeline.

China's youth are chatting and flirting online. As elsewhere across the globe, the internet is changing their lives. From around 9 million users in 1999, there were over 591 million users by July 2013. This makes China the country with the largest number of internet users in the world. The US came in second in the same year, with 254 million users, while India, its gargantuan neighbour, was third, with 152 million. A year later, China added another 41 million users, taking the number to 632 million internet users by summer 2014. The vast majority of these are under the age of 30 and therefore the ramifications of life online are most felt by the young of China. This can be seen in the Chinese lexicon alone. As a nation obsessed by food, whether feasting or – decades ago – simply fighting off starvation, a common greeting in China is *'Ni chi le ma?'* – 'Have you eaten?' Around the year 2000, young people started to instead ask, *'Ni shang wang le ma?'* – 'Have you been on the net yet?' That is how important the internet has become in Chinese daily life.

Social media is the height of connectivity and here once again China has surged ahead. Even though the likes of Facebook and Twitter have been blocked in China for some time, this has done little to stop the spread of indigenous social media. In fact, the blocking of the US internet giants has been to the benefit of Chinese. Chinese internet companies have made big bucks from copying Western models, while a neighbourhood of Beijing called Zhongguancuan has been nicknamed China's Silicon Valley and is teeming with companies trying to get a slice of a huge audience.

Blogs have particular appeal to the Chinese market. With journalism being a tightly controlled profession, the internet is one of the few spaces where young people can really make their voices heard. Censorship is a factor in Chinese cyberspace, but it is not quite as strict as outsiders often assume. According to a study conducted from Harvard University in 2012, scathing criticism of the regime and its leaders was tolerated online if the criticism was unlikely to lead to collective action. The censors, thousands of men and women employed by the government to monitor the web daily, are most concerned with online activity that can escalate beyond control. Individual criticism and comments on small-scale protests are fine, since they are unlikely to disturb China's 'harmonious society'. In one example in the study, a blogger described the city government as being 'without justice' and one that 'trades dignity for power', amongst other negative slurs. Pretty biting, yet with no hint of collective intent it remained uncensored.

Meanwhile, seemingly innocent non-political posts are sometimes deleted. Following the Japanese earthquake and the subsequent meltdown of the Fukushima nuclear plant, a rumour spread through Zhejiang Province that iodine salt would counteract radiation exposure. To stop a hectic rush to buy the salt, all online content relating to this rumour was removed.

It is not just in terms of freedom of expression that the internet is changing Chinese lives. The sexual landscape is constantly being renavigated online too. Naked chat rooms (*luoliao*) are perhaps the greatest example of the freedom of the net, or at least the government's inability to control all within its borders. This practice, while not widespread, involves literally talking naked. Usually heads are not revealed, nor are real names, and the chat rooms are controlled by passwords.

Pornography itself is still off limits in China, having been banned back in 1949 when Mao first came to power. He deemed it an impure element in society, a sentiment that continued under Deng Xiaoping, who in 1988 was quoted in the Chinese media as saying that some publishers of pornography should be executed.

Of course these measures have done nothing to stop the proliferation of pornography. For example, many Cultural Revolution memoirs from those who were sent to work in the country feature stories of enjoying erotic literature and porn. The internet has now become the latest and biggest battleground. Words that relate to sexual acts and erotica are blocked from search engines. Thousands of websites are shut down every year. And yet despite this, pornography is still very easy to find.

ONLINE DATING WITH CHINESE CHARACTERISTICS

One area that the government is keen to nurture online is the dating market. The internet has been a godsend for many singles in China. As recently as 1990, researchers found that a vast majority of residents in two of China's largest cities dated just one person before marriage: their prospective spouse. China's transition to a market economy has swept away many restrictions in people's lives. People now typically date more than one person before marriage. But, of all the new sexual and romantic freedoms the Chinese enjoy, seeking a partner is unexpectedly complicated and still proves difficult for rich and poor, young and old alike. Not content to leave matters up to fate or park-frequenting parents, online dating has therefore become a fallback for many singles in China.

China now has a plethora of platforms. Momo, for example, is a mobile app offering location-based matchmaking. It can be likened to Tinder, the US dating app known for easy hook-ups, only for people who like emoticons (in my experience these are a turn-on in China and a turn-off elsewhere). Recently it's branched out from matchmaking to offer a more conventional dating and socialising service. No doubt this is partly fuelled by pragmatism, a desire to keep people using the app even if they are in a relationship. It also shows how the quests for love and friendship in China are intertwined. The country's singles can be a lonely bunch.

At the more 'traditional' end of the spectrum, dating sites have sprung up by the dozen. Their ascent has been remarkable. It has been barely a decade since Gong Haiyan, a singleton from Shanghai, started the online date site Jiayuan.com ('Beautiful Destiny') in 2003. Allegedly, she was frustrated by the lack of legitimate dating options around her. The bare-bones website she initially sketched out has since grown into China's largest online dating site.

China might have been late to the game; in the West the first ever dating sites are believed to be Kiss.com and Match.com, founded by the same person in 1994 and 1995, respectively. But this slow start has not stopped online dating from taking off big time. It's estimated that 3 million paying customers signed up online in 2012, who collectively spent more than £100 million. Jiayuan alone had 63 million subscribers by 2012. Earning more than 44 per cent of the Chinese online dating sector's revenue, Jiayuan soon went public and is now NASDAQ listed.

Jiayuan's rival, Zhenai, has nearly 30 million users (in comparison, Match.com, one of the largest online dating websites in the US, has 15 million users). These numbers are growing: Zhenai maintains a 40 per cent annual growth rate. For this reason, IAC, Match.com's major shareholder, has bought a 20 per cent stake in Zhenai.

Like their foreign counterparts, Chinese websites allow subscribers to create online profiles, browse listings of thousands of potential partners around the country, chat online and send virtual gifts. They can also attend offline mix-and-mingle events with like-minded singles for a monthly fee. For a little more, the websites offer targeted matchmaking services and will arrange dates for members without the time or inclination to browse through the thousands of profiles of singles. A six-month membership on Jiayuan – which costs more than half the average wage for the same period in Beijing – buys users all of this, alongside feedback and advice.

Superficially it all sounds quite familiar to us. If you look a little closer, though, some remarkable differences between the average dating site in China and its Western equivalents emerge, starting with the basic information section. Some of the standard questions are asked the world over: height, weight and age. After that online daters in China demand a lot more detail. It is not enough to say you are slim. Instead you have to say how many kilos you weigh precisely. Nor is it enough to say just your age; you need to list your month of birth, alongside both your Chinese and Western star sign. Horoscopes matter – it is commonplace to hear, particularly amongst females, sentences peppered with references to the zodiac. Another thing that you must list, because it too is linked to personality, is blood type. My co-workers in Beijing almost called an emergency meeting when they discovered I was O negative. Type Os are ambitious and confident, apparently. As for the negative, I was said to be so rare that they joked I was some sort of spy planted in China by the UK royal family, members of whom also allegedly share my blood type.

Blood type and body mass are just the starting points. There are also the deal makers and breakers: exact monthly salary and whether you own a house or a car. Having a *hukou* – a resident permit – is also a big draw. In China, having a residency permit in a top-tier city is highly desirable because only those with permits have access to all the public services and certain social and employment opportunities in that city. If you marry someone with a Beijing *hukou*, your life will be much easier – sort of like marrying a US passport holder to facilitate a green card, though on a much more entrenched scale; Beijing's migrant workers, for example, are heavily disadvantaged in the marriage market for this very reason.

Finally, people are asked their ethnicity. China officially has 56 ethnic groups, with Han Chinese representing the biggest – some 92 per cent of the total population. These groups can be defined according to a host of factors, from language and culture to religion and region. Tibetan, Hui and Uyghur are the three most prominent, though not the most populous (the Zhuang claim that spot). Given the disparities in experience and identity between the groups, some will happily marry people from other ethnicities; others will not.

As with online dating in the West, a personalised introduction is also an important part of the profile. For those with writer's block, Zhenai provides an example:

> Before, in order to focus on my studies, my mum didn't let me date. Now, because of work, I don't have time to date. As time passed, I suddenly discovered I'd already become one of the 'sheng nu.' Actually my demands for my other half aren't that high. He doesn't have to be that handsome, or that wealthy, but he must be motivated, responsible, obedient, and that's about all. I have great hopes and visions for my future, but I hope to accomplish them with the person I love.

As the tone indicates, these sites are for the more marriage-minded. The primary players in this space – Jiayuan, Zhenai and Baihe – advertise themselves explicitly as marriage websites focused on helping singles find their future life partner. And therefore, once your profile has been uploaded and photos selected, there is one final task: each user has to check a box affirming their good moral character and honest intention to search for a spouse on the site. Those in the market for a simple one-night stand should head to a karaoke or massage parlour and pay for it.

This moral tick-box also hints at another issue. On a par with the rapid growth in the number of users, the number of cases of fraud has increased on dating websites. The year 2011 saw a female user suing Jiayuan after she was swindled by a man she had met on the website. Many other forms of fraud, ranging from publishing fake salary information to prostitution, have tarnished the reputation of dating websites. To solve this, Jiayuan has introduced a function enabling users to be blacklisted and, on occasion, requires validation from an employer's human resources department if a user's salary increases dramatically.

Perhaps the most prevalent form of cheating is doctored images, or even outright fake ones. This is not simply a case of selecting photos of yourself from five years ago or ones taken from a particularly flattering angle, but rather choosing photos of someone else entirely. In Leslie T. Chang's powerful and touching book *Factory Girls*, she chronicles just how ubiquitous cheating online is when some of the young girls she is following, factory-workers in the southern city of Dongguan, see no issue in using faking photos to attract men. They choose pictures of pretty girls, reasoning that it is better to get them on a date and then woo them with their personalities rather than not secure a date at all.

This example further illustrates how difficult people can find meeting other people in modern China. It also highlights how the pendulum has shifted in recent years. For the generation born before 1949, marriages were often arranged and therefore out of their control. A well-matched family background was important, not whether or not the couple would find each other physically attractive. This is not to say that appearance was not valued. Certainly for women it was, but in traditional China roles were delineated: men were meant to nurture talent out of the house in terms of professional achievement and women inner beauty over ability and outward appearance. A saying went, 'a virtuous woman is one without talents' (*nuzi wu cai bian shi de*). Beautiful women could be mistresses; wives were about something else.

Likewise, under the Communists before the 1980s, appearance was not high up on the list of matrimonial requirements. Marriages were arranged in a different way – according to good Communist values.

In today's market economy, it's a dog eat dog world. Two popular Chinese sayings show what women are expected to bring to the table. One goes, 'a talented man matches with a beautiful woman' (*lang cai nu mao*), and another, 'a woman dolls herself up for the man who loves her' (*nu wei yuejizhe rong*). As it was before, a woman's presentation is still more important than her talent. Unlike before, if she fails to live up to a certain level of attractiveness, she might fail to attract suitors.

It's no surprise then that the beauty industry is flourishing. Wen Hua exposes the extent of the industry in her book *Buying Beauty: Cosmetic Surgery in China*, where she highlights just how much cosmetic surgery has risen. This is in part motivated by career aspirations. Certain jobs expect women to look a certain way, even if their appearance has very little to do with the role at hand. It's not atypical for job ads to demand women to be of a certain height and appearance, and many women who Wen interviewed cited job competitiveness as a motivation for getting surgery. Others did so to become more attractive in the hope of finding a husband.

While it is predominantly women investing in the beauty industry, men aren't completely removed from pressure to look a certain way. Metrosexuality has taken off in China, as evidenced through a meander around some of Beijing's many shopping districts. 'City jade man' (*dushi yu nan*) describes a Chinese man who pays attention to his appearance and is effeminate. 'City-style man' (*dushi xing nan*), 'neuter pretty man' (*dushi zhongxing mei nan*), 'flowery man' (*hua mei nan*) and 'post-yuppie' (*hou yapi*) are similar terms.

Some outsiders assume that these young men and women are working to Western beauty ideals, the market for double eyelid surgery and white skin being signifiers. This is an over-simplified interpretation. A distinctly Chinese, or at least Asian, aesthetic is emerging. Where the commonality between the West and China lies is that beauty is increasingly becoming something unattainable and expensive, and this is driving insecurities about people's looks, online and off.

ONE CHINESE GIRL'S BATTLE WITH ONLINE DATING

Shu, a pretty 26-year-old recruitment consultant from Hubei with a heart-shaped face and long, shiny black hair, had done everything by the book. She had met a guy at college and after a couple of years had moved in with him. Their relationship had lasted for four years and was very serious. His parents had even made the 20-hour train journey from their hometown to her parents' to discuss the couple's future – the clearest sign of commitment in any Chinese relationship.

However, Shu fell out of love with him when she realised that his main priorities were not aligned with her own. His were straightforward: make money and get married. Hers were less so: 'He didn't support me much. He's a traditional Chinese guy. He thinks I am below him because I am a girl. I am allowed to have fun but not be serious,' Shu says, explaining how she wanted to be an entrepreneur, while he wanted her to be a housewife.

> He was poor. Before I met him I would spend lots of money travelling. But he had little and thought what little he had he would just spend on his girlfriend. During the four years we were together I travelled nowhere, except for work.

When she mooted the idea of breaking up to her parents they were unsupportive. From the outside, to a Chinese parent, he took good care of her, doing most of the cooking and cleaning at home, and he was on a good trajectory, having studied at Tsinghua and gone on to make lots of money.

'My parents would say, "How did you find such a subservient man from Tsinghua? You can't find a top 1 per cent to do all of this",' she adds laughing.

One per cent or not, he was not right and she walked away. For the first time in years, Shu found herself single and alone. She had just relocated to Beijing and knew very few people. She would literally cry into her noodles, she says, recounting the horror.

Shu tells me about this in one of Beijing's many Starbucks. She is laughing, pulling her long hair, making all kinds of movements to dramatise the story. We are sitting squished on a sofa next to a businessman, who occasionally shoots us a disparaging look. It is another busy Starbucks, one of a multitude around the city. Despite Beijingers earning around five-and-a-half times less on average than their equivalents in the UK, and Starbucks charging a lot for coffee, Beijing is littered with coffee chain outlets, all of which are always full. Of course the nation still spends plenty of time (and money) guzzling green, jasmine, *pu'er* and other traditional leaves, but the bean has infiltrated the nation very successfully. Starbucks estimates China will be its second-biggest market, after the US, by 2015.

With Shu newly single, her housemate decided to enrol her on two dating sites. He was working as a creative director at Jiayuan and Baihe and deemed a VIP account a perfect break-up tonic. Shu listed her criteria as someone tall and older with a degree. She stated that she wanted him to be earning not only more than her in the present but more than her calculations of her future earnings when she would get to his age, a sign of the traditional mindset of even the more modern clientele.

Within a few weeks of being online, she had lined up several dates. The first was with a technology worker who took her to KFC. Western fast-food outlets do not have quite the same reputation as they do in the West. Fast food in China is relatively expensive compared to local fare, and visiting them is seen as buying into an American lifestyle, which for the upwardly mobile is highly desirable. As a result, the way the restaurants are used is entirely different. In the West people do not linger; in China a visit can last hours. It is more than acceptable to take a date to one. Weddings have even been held at KFC, which is by far the biggest Western success story in China.

Her first date seemed honest and nice and Shu soon set up a second date. In the interim, they chatted every day on the phone. I hesitantly asked her if there was a kiss at the end of the first date, given the intensity of chatting daily after it.

'No! The Chinese style is very slow. If we kiss it means we are already boyfriend and girlfriend.'

It is hard to tell if this conservatism is a national trend, though there is evidence to support it. From my personal experience at least: I once kissed a Chinese guy on the first night I met him, who then proceeded to call me his girlfriend and say he felt 'very protective of' me. Kissing is seen as quite forward in China.

The second man she met online was the big catch, a really handsome director at his own start-up IT company. He was a member of the prestigious Toastmasters, a global communications and leadership corporation, a fact which deeply impressed her at the time. He was funny, likable and international. She gushes:

> At that time I was just a stupid girl. I would sit at home and watch Korean TV. I was so impressed. He seemed so fashionable, international and stylish. Tough but not so tough. Sexy tough. Ahhhh, you can see clearly many people like him. He even had a blog and lots of girls would leave comments.

When Shu met him, he was even better looking in real life. Were his looks important to her? For the most part, no. Like many Chinese girls, she was not motivated by physical attraction so much as the other aspects of his personality that he presented. If anything, his looks and confidence unnerved her and the date was short.

For their third date he invited her over to his. She was nervous to go since she still hardly knew him, so she got her friend who lived nearby to drive her and wait outside in case anything happened. In Beijing, it is often assumed that the streets are relatively safe; the incidence of sexual assault is portrayed as low compared to other countries (it's hard to substantiate this due to the government tightly controlling statistics). A different story emerges off the streets and inside the homes. In a 2013 survey carried out by the UN, 50 per cent of Chinese men said they had physically or sexually abused their partners. Like other women who meet men online elsewhere in the world, Shu was therefore wise to take precautions.

When Shu felt more confident in his house and company, she gave her friend the go-ahead to leave. They then played Chinese chess and in the middle of the game he leant over to kiss her.

'It was unsuccessful. I liked him but felt he didn't like me and I didn't want to be a toy.'

Once again it's hard to tell how normal Shu's 'pace' was, and following on from this, how long Chinese people usually take to sleep together. The conversations I have had or overheard with Chinese people are generally less lascivious than back home, but then talking about something and doing something are two very different things.

CASUAL SEX IN BEIJING

Foreign nationals living in Beijing will commonly report that the Chinese people they have been with are just as comfortable with casual sex as we have become in the West. However, this is not necessarily a reliable group: the people they sleep with might be much more in touch with Western norms and therefore unrepresentative of Chinese people as a whole. This group of Chinese people also might have preconceptions about foreigners sexually and change their behaviour accordingly. I know of several examples of Chinese girls sleeping with foreigners where the girl's behaviour is in direct relation to their perceptions of foreign girls. One texted a male former housemate of mine, saying she didn't want a boyfriend like Chinese girls do and instead if he went on a date with her, she would have sex with him at the end, like a foreign girl. Another male friend who dated a Chinese girl for some time confided how his girlfriend was hyper-aware of the disparities between Western and Chinese girls in bed, constantly demanding comparisons.

In his book *Behind the Red Door: Sex in China*, Richard Burger quotes Professor Li Yinhe, an expert on family and marriage from the Chinese Academy of Social Science, who said in an interview in 2010 that more than 60 per cent of urban Chinese had sex before marriage, compared to only 15 per cent in 1989. More recent statistics – from 2012 – place the figure at 70 per cent. That still means that 30 per cent do not partake in premarital sex, as opposed to the US, where the proportion of abstainers is way below 5 per cent. And for China's virgins, it's not religion motivating them (though religion is growing in importance, as will be outlined later). Rather it's the heavy hand of tradition stipulating that women must remain chaste to remain eligible.

As Burger explains, 'virginity still matters in China.' He cites the prevalence of sex stores selling fake hymens as evidence, and hospitals and clinics also offer hymen-repair surgery, both of which suggest that if young Chinese are having premarital sex, they aren't yet comfortable with its ramifications.

It's no surprise that China's youth are still uneasy with sex. They hear conflicting messages in the Chinese media, some promoting it and some against it. In 2011 Bai Wanqing, a Shanghai People's Congress deputy, stirred controversy when she proclaimed: 'Virginity is the most precious dowry a girl can give to her husband's family.' This was around the same time that Tu Shiyou, a 38-year-old single woman from Hubei Province, launched a website called Preserve Virginity. As the title implies, it promotes sexual abstinence before marriage. Tu's website lists the physical and psychological damage that a woman might succumb to by having premarital sex, such as sexually transmitted diseases and unwanted pregnancies.

'Conserving virginity has positive social effects and holds great value for both men and women. You can protect yourself through chastity,' she says on her site.

While Tu directs her message at men as well as women, it is still the latter who are cautioned the most against premarital sex. A 2010 survey by China's largest online network, qq.com, showed that more than 80 per cent of the 160,000 male respondents wanted to marry a virgin, while only 13 per cent said it didn't matter. The most sobering example took place in Hebei Province in 2010 when a 23-year-old newly wed woman was stabbed by her husband after he discovered she was not a virgin.

And yet Chinese men still expect sex from their partners. With marriage ages rising, some women who choose to wait either have to avoid steady relationships altogether or face abusive pressure from the men they date. Women are therefore damned if they do and damned if they don't.

The jury is still out when it comes to questions of promiscuity and how normal or not sex is. What seems to be reasonable is that the truth lies somewhere in between: Beijingers, at least, are more open to multiple sexual partners and sex before marriage in ways their parents and grandparents were not, but they are still less promiscuous than twenty-somethings in other major capital cities, and they are still not entirely comfortable with premarital sex as a concept.

In the end Shu gave her date a kiss goodnight, after he tried once again at the subway station. However, after several more weeks of game playing she grew tired and uncertain of his intentions. Two years later their paths crossed again. This time he was a lot more attentive and she was feeling more secure about herself and felt they could be a better, more even match, so she asked if she could be his girlfriend. He said he had too much work and travel, and was generally very evasive. On one of these trips he called and announced he was divorced.

'When did you get married?' she asked.

'Last year.'

'When did you get divorced?'

'Last year.'

Apparently he had forgotten the part of the online dating form where he vouched for his good character. Shu was forced once again to walk away.

THE RISE OF THE LIGHTNING DIVORCE

Shu had just dated a statistic, that of the lightning divorcees. The incidence of young couples getting married and divorced in quick succession is a rising trend – a fascinating one when you consider its wider implications. One in every five marriages in China now ends in divorce, with Beijing accounting for almost 39 per cent of the total. Statistics are particularly striking amongst the nation's only children. Information from a Beijing district court in 2009 showed that the divorce rate amongst the under-thirties had doubled annually since 2004, with 97 per cent of divorcees being only children. How did China, a country that places family values foremost, get to this place?

Different reasons have been proposed. One is that in this increasingly materialistic world, the desire to trade up is strong. It's the irony of the pressure to marry – people are rushing into marriage and realising their mistake later. Another reason is that molly-coddled only children find self-sufficiency and compromise difficult, leading to conflict not easily resolved within matrimony.

Divorce is also easier to obtain. Although it was made legal for the first time under Chairman Mao in the 1950s, couples still needed permission from their work unit to obtain a divorce, right up until 2002. It might seem surprising that the workforce should exert so much control over the private lives of its workers, but it should be noted that even today couples still need permission from their boss to have a child. China is not a country where work life and private life are easily separated.

One final reason attributed to the rise in divorce rates is the fact that divorce has shed a lot of its stigma. Divorce is a lot more socially acceptable in the new millennium than before. Second-hand male suitors also do surprisingly well in the marriage market. A 2013 survey of over 35,500 single women offers some insight into their attitudes towards divorce. When asked, 'What kind of men are you willing to marry?' the most popular response was 'a divorced man who owns a house and car,' followed by 'a successful forty-something man who has gone on a lot of blind dates but is still single.'

Not all feel comfortable with the label, though, as Shu's story illustrates. She didn't like the idea of dating a divorcee, which shows that even if divorce has shed some of its stigma and is becoming more prominent, China still holds tightly to its conservative family values. That said, like many young urban Chinese, Shu has been forced by her dating experiences to reconsider some of her own prejudices and values. They've changed her, and might change the fabric of China's relationships in the future. She tells me, smiling:

> I was so serious wanting to find a boyfriend to marry over the past two years and yet I found nothing. I feel I've changed a lot. I used to think that a girlfriend and boyfriend should meet every day. Now I know I need to have fun by myself and be independent. I'm no longer like a traditional Chinese girl. I now live in the moment more. If you go to the pool, you need to learn to swim by yourself. Before I was reliant on a float.

It's apparent from talking to Shu and others who have experienced online dating that even if Chinese girls still feel pushed to settle down, not all are giving in to the pressure. With more freedom and choice over who to wed, people are becoming pickier, starting to look for 'the one', the person with whom they have that 'magic spark', a Western mentality which is taking hold in China.

It comes as no surprise then that just as the internet is facilitating matchmaking, it is also facilitating the opposite: sites offering break-up services (literally people whom you pay to do your own dirty work) are another example of how love is playing to new rules in China and creating alternative options. The increase in choice is having ramifications in people's personal lives in other ways too. Shu, for instance, is very excited about having set up her own company, something she felt discouraged from doing by the men in her life. She is not the only one playing her cards differently. These newly independent young people have a chance to influence a real change in attitude. In urban areas, many women are learning to be independent and to take control over their prospects in life, as we'll see later in the book. First, though, I would like to introduce the women who are still putting money ahead of other factors when it comes to matrimony.

3

Diamond Love
China's Rich Kids and who they Date

I want to be an alpha male.
Jiang, attendee at the Lijiang Plan course

Chinese men continue to enjoy a privileged position in society. However, even at the top, there are winners and there are losers, at least when it comes to love. The so-called 'phoenix man' is among the latter. Broadly defined, a phoenix man is someone who has climbed his way up from humble beginnings. Instead of being hailed as heroes who changed their fate, 'phoenix men' have long been unpopular in the Chinese marriage market, especially among another category: 'peacock girls' – women from urban, relatively wealthy families. This demographic is turned off by the phoenix man's supposed insecurity, fear of failure, penny pinching and prioritisation of extended family over an immediate one. These are believed to be traits irreversibly ingrained in their mentality by the time they reach adulthood.

Validating people's desire to separate 'true gold' from 'new gold' are several courses on offer in the country. A school in Beijing called the Moral Education Centre teaches women how to date and marry a millionaire. Learning to decipher a man's character and status is a central part of the curriculum.

IN SEARCH OF A PRINCE

Huang doesn't need a course to tell her how to win the right man. She just needs the right man. She was born into the more privileged end of China's social spectrum, yet is far from being rich and believes that life will be easier with money. How to get it, or rather who to date, is her current focus.

I meet her at a restaurant in one of Beijing's trendiest traditional lanes. It is an evocative venue, one where I had dined in July 2012, on the day of Beijing's notorious storms which caused the biggest floods the city had experienced in over 60 years. On a macro scale, thousands died and hundreds of buildings were damaged, as Beijing's drainage system failed to accommodate the level of rain and the city quickly filled up like a blocked kitchen sink. On a personal, micro level, part of the ceiling of the restaurant I was in collapsed. Many months later, there is no sign of the damage that day caused, but a brief power cut hints at a city infrastructure that is still struggling to keep up with the country's surge towards modernity.

Huang arrives a little late, with a colleague in tow. The pair work at one of China's biggest banks and look like typical white-collar workers, both smartly dressed. At the same time, Huang clearly has an eye for fashion. She's wearing trendy wide-rimmed glasses and her nails sparkle at the tips with silver glitter, a very modern Chinese aesthetic. They sit down and deliberate over the menu for a while, reading out every single choice. Huang strokes it with her shimmering fingers. 'We're both Gemini,' her colleague jokes in explanation for their lack of decision-making. I raise a cynical eyebrow at the mention of astrology. It is about the third reference to star signs I have heard that day.

Huang is attractive in an understated way. With the exception of the nails, she's wearing minimal makeup and her long hair is scraped back into a bun. She has a bubbly voice and it soon becomes clear that she is a keen narrator.

She arrived in Beijing a few years back, having completed a degree in journalism at Chongqing University, in China's south-central Sichuan Province, and made the switch to banking out of a sense of pragmatism rather than passion.

'It's a sad story. I gave up my major because it's a state-owned bank. It has better pay than journalism jobs and it gives you *hukou*,' she says, talking of the resident permit that plagues people in China, tying them down to a particular locale through granting social services only to *hukou* permit holders. *Hukou* is a golden ticket. 'If you don't have *hukou* and you live in Beijing, you can't buy an apartment, and rents are high. It just makes life easier. We have to face the reality and pressure of life here,' she says, matter-of-factly.

The other girl nods in agreement, explaining this often happens: young people sacrificing dreams for a piece of paper. Of course one can manipulate the system. They have a former colleague who upon graduating from Peking University, accepted a position at their company just to get a *hukou*. Once it was secured, he quickly changed jobs to one with better pay. This too occurs frequently. Workforce retention is an issue in China. Young Chinese will move around quickly if they can improve their situation. From my experience of working in a Chinese company (and I have heard it is fairly representative), bosses do little to foster a sense of loyalty to the company. The approach is more stick than carrot. A re-evaluation might be in order soon, to keep pace with the evolution of China's workforce – gone are the days of a seemingly endless supply of cheap, undemanding labour.

Huang has stuck at her job and will continue to do so until something better comes along. Ideally this something would be a man. 'I'm a realist,' is a line peppering the conversation we have. She admits that she doesn't need a partner. She earns a decent wage and can fend for herself. She just wants one.

It was with this in mind that she ended up on a date with a *fu'erdai*. The *fu'erdai* represent another face of modern China. The word is a colloquialism that literally translates as 'rich second generation'. It refers to the children whose parents made their money under Deng Xiaoping, the first leader after Mao, who is credited with launching the country's economic turnaround.

Fu'erdai has become an umbrella term for all of China's 'trust-fund kids' and can be divided into three distinct groups. The first are the *guan'erdai*, meaning 'government official second generation'. The second, *xing'erdai*, are the 'super-star second generation'. The third, *hong'erdai*, are the children whose families have strong roots in the Communist Party.

While some of this generation's parents secured a privileged position under Mao through aligning themselves closely to the Communist elite, the translation of their connections into cash is part of the narrative of the opening-up period. Out of the economic turnaround arose the *fu'erdai*. Bo Guagua, the son of Bo Xilai, former champion of China's New Left, was, until his father's spectacular fall from grace, the poster boy of the *fu'erdai*, all good looks and a top Western education. He is one of the many who attend the world's top boarding schools and colleges, the people who often appear in photos published in both Western and Chinese media sources queuing outside Harrods and other top department stores. Within China, plenty of these sons and daughters have become household names, in much the same way that Paris Hilton and Nicole Richie have in the West. Members of Sports Car Club (SCC) are perhaps the most famous, or rather infamous, and provide a sense of just how wealthy some of these kids are.

The SCC was first formed in 2009 as a simple car enthusiast club and quickly became synonymous with the *fu'erdai*, a reputation cemented when its membership roster surfaced online, revealing that most of the 11 members of the club were *fu'erdai*, whose net worth was over 10 billion yuan (£1 billion).

That the SCC is populated by China's elite is hardly a surprise given that in order to join, people need to pay a sizable annual membership fee and, most importantly, have access to an unbelievably expensive sports car. Entry-level sports cars barely make the cut. A brand-new Porsche might stop an application from being instantly thrown in the trash, but if you want to secure membership you really need to own metal worth millions. Most of the members are below the age of 30 and some have collected over ten sports cars.

Huang's *fu'erdai* – not a member of the SCC himself – does have a Porsche and other trappings of extreme wealth. The match was made through her uncle, who suggested they meet in a luxury hotel for their first date.

'It was a scary experience. The hotel intimidated me. No one chooses such a luxury place for a first date. But it was okay, I accept that is the *fu'erdai* way.'

If the hotel was intimidating, Huang was in for an even bigger shock. She was greeted at the entrance by her date, who then led her through the gargantuan lobby and into a private room of the restaurant. There, in the middle of a very traditional Chinese setting, sat his mother, drinking tea.

'She was sitting there like a queen, drinking tea so elegantly and slowly. I was already scared and she made me even more nervous. I hardly ate and definitely made sure to make no sounds while I did,' Huang tells me, imitating her mannerisms.

Throughout the dinner the mother fired questions at her, about her employment history, family background and so on. Huang likened the date to an interview. While never entirely certain why the mother came along, Huang has her suspicions: 'I think two reasons. First, he is from a big, important family. So it matters who he dates. And second, his mother is an important, strong person.'

I also have my suspicions, namely that the mother would be aware of clichés about Chinese women wanting to marry for money and therefore keen to protect their assets. A controversial recent change to marriage legislation reflects just how deep these suspicions run. Now if Chinese people get divorced, whoever initially bought the house or apartment that they shared gets to keep it entirely, even if the other party put in a lot of money in terms of decorations and mortgage payments. It's been labelled the law that makes men laugh and women cry, as it is often the men who own the house.

The ruling has been justified with the argument that it shores up the unstable institution of marriage by making divorce less attractive, and that it attempts to stop women marrying with the wrong intentions. The perceptions are that a woman could refuse to marry a man if he does not come with a home. It is deemed such a custom that tying the knot with a man who doesn't own a property is named a 'naked wedding'. As stories like these circulate, they feed the misconception that women are marrying simply because they want to guarantee half of a house in the event of divorce. This perception is not backed up by the reality on the ground and therefore all the law has done is place women in a very compromised position.

To circumvent the law, some women have told their fiancés that they will refuse to have children, or care for their partner's parents – the traditional duty of wives in China – unless they are registered as the co-owner of the property before they marry. That is the only way to guarantee they can legally keep half of the home, and even then it can be complicated. The truth is that the new law has left many wives with landlords for husbands, and those who seek divorce are walking away with nothing to show for their years of marriage. There is also a fear that it has encouraged the already rampant mistress culture, as women's bargaining tool of taking half the house has been removed.

The UK, by contrast, recognises the nuances of home ownership and awards both parties justly. Moreover, property is not intrinsically tied to masculinity, as is the case in China, where it means that women are often becoming their own executioners, allowing men to walk away with more in order to avoid tension. Families aggravate the situation; both sides apply pressure to ensure money is directed away from women and towards men.

Huang was not at the stage of discussing property with her *fu'erdai* and their relationship went no further. She left with a good impression and one which challenged conventional wisdom about China's rich kids. 'He was a nice guy. He seemed both sunny and funny, not like a typical *fu'erdai*. Not spending money like crazy.'

Huang went on a few more dates with him. On one of the dates he drove her around in his Porsche. On each date the mother was present, either in person or on the phone. Overbearing mothers are quite normal in China, particularly where sons are concerned. A common joke goes that a girl should never ask her boyfriend who he would save first if she fell into a lake with his mother. Girls are told that if they want to be the number-one woman in a man's life, they have to wait until they have a son of their own. So Huang is used to the idea of marrying someone whose parents would come as a main part of the package. She is very close to her family too. Her aunt and grandmother both live in Beijing and proximity to her grandmother is the main reason she moved from south to north. In fact, despite a hefty workload and social life, Huang visits her grandmother every week, staying overnight to spend as much free time with her as possible. Like other Chinese kids, she was raised by her grandmother until she went to primary school as neither of her parents were around; her father was actually at university to make up for the degree he was denied during the Cultural Revolution. She is closer to her grandmother than she is to her mother.

The deal-breaker for Huang and her *fu'erdai* was not his mother; it was his admission that he was in no particular rush to get married. At the age of 26 and female, Huang felt differently. She called things off with him and moved on.

'At least this guy was good,' Huang reflects. 'I had so many other dates that were terrible.' She talks of one specifically where she went out with a guy who was in the military intelligence branch of the People's Liberation Army. He was boring and ugly, she says, with yellow, crooked teeth. 'He was too tanned too,' she adds, the class snobbishness coming across. Tanning salons are making a slow debut in China, as the nation continues to obsess over white skin and associate dark skin with poor people whose only choice is to work outside in the fields.

Huang's positive memories are at odds with the usual associations of *fu'erdai*, which are much more negative. The members of the SCC have received bad press over the years. On top of driving envy-inducing cars, they also party hard. And when they party it is extravagant. There have been allegations of events attended by *fu'erdai* featuring high-class prostitutes, drugs and thousands of condoms. Another example of conspicuous consumption involved 22-year-old Zhang Jiale, the daughter of Sino Life Insurance boss Zhang Jun, uploading a series of photos of herself flying in private jets and shopping for top designer brands onto Weibo. The images went viral, prompting a wave of jealousy and outrage from the general public, most of whom will never be rich.

It is not just their wealth that the *fu'erdai* flaunt; it is also their privilege. For example, in 2010 the 22-year-old Li Qiming, intoxicated and speeding in his luxury car, hit a college girl and killed her. When arrested, he allegedly shouted 'Go ahead, sue me if you dare. My father is Li Gang!' The phrase quickly went viral, becoming a popular internet catchphrase and meme within China, used to denote arrogance and shirking of responsibility.

More recently, in 2013 Li Tianyi, the 17-year-old son of famous Chinese general and singer Li Shuangjiang, who sang popular 'red songs' during the Cultural Revolution, was held for his involvement in a gang rape case. Hearing that he might go unpunished, an online storm ensued; many Chinese netizens saw his crime as proof that their negative feelings about privileged families were right, that they were above the law in Chinese society. Li had erred at the wrong time. China's new president, Xi Jinping, had vowed to crack down on corruption. Making a scapegoat of the occasional *fu'erdai* was an easy way to highlight the sincerity of his pledge. In the wake of Li's case, *People's Daily*, the most famous state-run media outlet, wrote:

> Multiple incidents involving '*keng die*' [children whose misdeeds have tarnished their fathers' reputations] have become hot-button issues in society, because of who they are and because of the violence or arrogance involved. Moreover, the era they live in is characterized by a public trust gap that stems from China's current class divisions, and we must build a bridge to re-build that trust.

Li was sentenced to ten years in jail, the maximum prison sentence for a juvenile.

Thus the *fu'erdai* represent a controversial group in China, seen as the embodiment of the country's ills just as much as of its success. Everyone has an opinion on them.

'The lives of the *fu'erdai* are so different to ours,' exclaims one vivacious mid-twenties woman I meet, who has only read about *fu'erdai*. Huang is in agreement, even if she remains attracted to the lifestyle and is more forgiving of the protagonists.

Even *fu'erdai* criticise *fu'erdai*. Wang Sicong, son of Dalian Wanda Group chairman Wang Jianlin – ranked by Forbes as the third-richest man in China – is a prolific blogger with 500,000 followers on Weibo. His account has become a launchpad for wars of words against other *fu'erdai*. Commenting on a photograph of an iPhone case produced by one member of the SCC, Wang wrote, 'Whoever says this looks good has eyes growing on their a**holes. Better to print, "I'm nouveau riche, I have no taste" instead.'

Wang draws distinctions between himself, a 'true' *fu'erdai*, and 'new money'. Not lacking in confidence online, Wang posts about the differences between *gaofushuai*, the 'tall, rich and handsome' youth of China – of which he rates himself an exemplar – and *diaosi* (literally 'pubic hairs'), meaning the unattractive college grads working dead-end jobs for minimal pay. Wang also refers to women who pursue *gaofushuai* by the anatomical slang term *heimu'er* (literally, wood ear mushroom). Sometimes his comments reveal self-awareness, such as when he posted, 'you don't understand the *gaofushuai* lifestyle,' next to a photo of two people in the backseat of a convertible in a rainstorm holding umbrellas up in lieu of putting up their roof. At other times his posts just act as an indication that a new class system is emerging in China. It's no longer enough just to have money; people now must have a degree of taste to be considered at the top of China's social system.

It's important to remind yourself when reading this that China is still first and foremost a Communist country founded on Communist principles. Only a generation ago, class warfare raged and anyone with inherited wealth or privilege was a target for persecution. Women could not even wear lipstick for fear of being labelled bourgeois and punished for such a crime. The *fu'erdai* show the U-turn China has made, all the while under the same banner of Communism. The government has called the recent change 'socialism with Chinese characteristics', but it's clear from the mixed reactions to the *fu'erdai* that people have reservations about the direction the country is heading in. In essence, the issue is larger than the people involved. As with most stereotypes and labels, *fu'erdai* serve as scapegoats for societal, economic and political ills. These rich kids and their exhibitionist ways are far easier targets than their parents, many of whom acquired their wealth in a controversial manner but are protected through their close connections to the government.

One thing's for certain about stereotypes: the reality is always a lot more colourful. I interviewed several *fu'erdai* and friends of *fu'erdai*. One guy specifically, who describes himself as a recent *fu'erdai* if pushed on the term, also draws a line between himself and other *fu'erdai* because 'he works hard and never receives money from his parents'.

He told me of his friend, also *fu'erdai*, a boy some ten years younger than him to whom he acts as a surrogate brother. He is very fond of this boy and believes he represents how misunderstood this section of Chinese youth are. The teenager – nicknamed 'Little Fatty' (*xiao pangzi*) because of his weight – is at times outrageous and attention seeking. On the evenings when they party together, he goes out with wads of cash, which he flashes at any given opportunity. On one occasion as much as 10,000 yuan was displayed as Little Fatty shouted loudly, 'I'm paying the bill, nobody move,' counting the money in front of everyone and picking up the tab for all those around him. On another occasion he went to Japan for a week just on a whim, where he spent 130,000 yuan (£13,000).

Despite this crude behaviour, his friend is keen to highlight that Little Fatty is hard-working, loyal and, more significantly, volunteers in the charity sector. He is part of a new generation increasingly aware of and interested in charity.

A report published by the China Charity and Donation Information Centre shows that charitable donations in China in 2012 were a paltry £8.8 billion, just 4 per cent of the total donations collected by charities in the US in the same time period. Those tightest with their money, according to a list published by luxury magazine *Hurun*, are China's super-wealthy. China now has more billionaires than the US. Despite this, only three of the ten most wealthy individuals made it onto the list of the top ten donors.

Charity has a chequered history in China, having been in fashion under certain dynasties such as the Ming and then very much out of fashion for most of the period of Communist rule. It is making a comeback, as the number of volunteers in the aftermath of the 2008 Sichuan earthquake show. At the same time, several individuals and incidents are tarnishing the reputation of the charitable sector. For example, in 2011 a young woman, Guo Meimei, who claimed to work for the Red Cross Society of China, was found flaunting her ostentatious lifestyle on social media, which hugely dented the reputation of the organisation.

Others don't give to charity since they simply cannot afford to. In a country where hundreds of millions still live below the poverty line, charity is not an option for most. This makes contributions from China's wealthiest all the more important. Yang Lan, China's version of Oprah, is on a mission to ensure that China's wealthy kids do just that. In 2010 Yang co-organised a banquet in Beijing with the Bill & Melinda Gates Foundation. Bill Gates and Warren Buffett were in attendance, to discuss philanthropy with more than 30 of China's billionaire families. A member of the National Committee of the Chinese People's Political Consultative Conference, Yang also proposed a law on philanthropy. Later at a private forum, she invited former US president Jimmy Carter and his wife to share their experiences of working in charity and to reveal their own thoughts on how China's charity sector could develop in a sustainable way.

'*Fu'erdai* or *guan'erdai*, those who inherited properties from their rich parents, are considered negative words. How do you turn *fu'erdai* or *guan'erdai* into *ci'erdai*, or those who promote education and build a culture of philanthropy in China?' Yang asked. *Ci'erdai* translates as 'second-generation philanthropists', and Yang sees these kids as the primary target in her quest for more charitable work.

The *fu'erdai* – in both what they represent and how they behave – have the power to make a difference to modern China on a social level. Whether they will do so has yet to be seen.

GETTING GAME: THE RICH MEN WHO NEED HELP DATING

Huang's former love interest is still on the prowl. As a wealthy, educated male, he feels no need to rush into marriage – and he's in good company. In stark contrast to China's educated females, who are told they must marry before the age of 27 or miss the boat, China's educated men are delivered different messages from the media. A 2013 survey conducted by matchmaking site Jiayuan said: 'Even though the wolves are many and the meat is little […] the vast majority of single men over 30 consider themselves to be in their golden years, without the slightest pressure [to marry].'

Even if some wealthy, educated men are more relaxed about marriage, the quest for love is still not easy – and causes them stress too. Finding the time and avenues to meet new people is tough for all in China's modern cities. Within this context bespoke matchmaking services have arisen to cater to the mega-rich, taking tips from companies in the West that have already sussed out how lucrative the luxury end of love is.

Amongst the better known is Golden Bachelor, an online dating site which caters to an expanding class of super-rich Chinese singletons who have everything except a girlfriend. The Golden Bachelor premium membership costs hundreds of thousands of yuan (tens of thousands of pounds). Requirements for joining are a personal or family wealth of at least 2 million yuan and a background that is superior and aristocratic, with good personal qualities. What exactly these mean is the territory of the consultants who work for the company; Golden Bachelor now has millions of registered members and employs psychologists and special matchmaking consultants to personally assist multimillionaires in their pursuit of romance.

Unlike the park love market we encountered earlier, which is an arena open to all, these matchmaking services pride themselves on their ability to lock out poorer prospects. For a hefty price tag, matchmakers will hunt down and vet prospective partners for wealthy clients. Their methods are ruthless. Like model scouts, they plant themselves in busy shopping districts waiting for attractive people to approach. Unlike model scouts, the judgement does not stop with appearance. The girls who are good-looking enough to make it through to the first stage go on to have their character scrutinised. Diamond Love and Marriage, another company, rates potentials on a scale of A, B and C, weighing up a plethora of factors.

If someone does secure a thumbs-up from a service, they are then made to undergo the biggest hurdle of them all – meeting the client and seeing if they can attract, and keep, their attention. One matchmaking company transported 200 would-be trophy wives to a resort town in south-western China for the perusal of one powerful magnate. Another organised a caravan of BMWs for rich businessmen to find young wives in Sichuan Province. Diamond Love sponsored a matchmaking event in 2009 where 21 men each paid an entrance fee close to £10,000. At these events, men largely take a backseat while the women – usually dressed to the nines – will try to prove their supposed eligibility in a way that more closely resembles a Miss World competition. They will sing, dance and cajole.

In some ways it is a modern twist on an old custom. Matchmakers have existed in China for over 2,000 years. Women have been paraded in front of men in a similar style throughout the centuries. Mistresses and concubines specifically were not valued just for their beauty; they were performers too. Ang Lee's movie *Lust, Caution* narrates the tale of a young woman who becomes a mistress to a Chinese collaborator during the

Sino-Japanese War in the 1930s. She seduces him through her ability to sing as much as her breathtaking good looks.

Yet, like other aspects of modern China, these matchmaking companies have been manipulated to fit the current climate. For centuries, when it came to marriage (as opposed to mistresses), the goal of matchmakers was usually to pair families of equal stature for the greater social good. There was even a term – *mendang hudui* – meaning roughly 'family doors of equal size'. In the modern era the rules have been changed as marriage has become a means to move up.

Plenty of *fu'erdai* are listed as clients. However, the ones who exert the biggest influence are the *fu'yidai* – the 'first-generation rich.' Well into their thirties or forties, age hasn't deterred them from wanting a young bride. Nor has the media, which constantly runs stories on younger women wanting older men. So what do these wealthy single men want? Alabaster skin, fine features, good character and, significantly, a 'pure' virgin are amongst the most commonly requested traits. As mentioned earlier, virgins are still valued highly in China. A double standard remains when it comes to men and women's sexual past. Though it seems to matter more to the less well-educated men who live in rural China, there are still plenty of urbanites who value virginity in prospective wives.

An added twist: Diamond Love and Marriage has female counterparts. Certain agencies promise to find wealthy women a perfect husband, such as Yali Marriage Quotient, which claims it can do it in three months (and that includes the whole wedding part too).

'We're more like an educational institute, offering classes that help women understand themselves better and build their confidence so they are more outgoing. Good things, including marriage, will happen once they start coming out of themselves,' explained life coach Liang Yali, the agency's founder, in an interview with *China Daily*. Liang said that the average time for 'graduation' is about 90 days, from the time the student starts classes to the day they walk down the aisle. She offers a 100 per cent refund if clients are unhappy.

Bigger matchmaking sites also offer bespoke services for the ultra-rich. Zhenai (meaning 'Cherish Love' in English) is one. A decent deposit buys members six months of personalised attention from one of the company's hundreds of matchmakers, who work in a call centre in the southern city of Shenzhen. The matchmakers advise men and women on how to tweak their profiles, what to wear to dinner, even how to fix their hair based on a large database of empirical evidence collected from members who have been asked out on a second date or not.

'For example, we find most men like women who wear black pantyhose,' Li, the founder, once said in an interview with CNN. 'It is overwhelming. So we tell them you don't have to do that, but these are the statistics.'

A PICK-UP ARTIST SHAKES THINGS UP

Dating services are not the only players angling for some of the booming love business. Chris 'Tango' Wu, a 26-year-old self-styled 'professional pick-up artist', also wants in.

Tango makes his money from teaching successful pick-up tricks to single male students who deem themselves unsuccessful in love. The students pay a premium rate to attend Tango's intensive training sessions that last from three days to a full week and feature classroom-style lectures followed by practical experience.

That his services have been so successful comes as no surprise to Tango, who notes that rising standards of affluence, combined with the social stigma of being single, have driven demand for creative solutions to problems of the heart.

'When a man has enough food to eat, water to drink and air to breathe, the next thing he needs to find is a woman,' Tango said in an interview about the success of his company. 'A man in his thirties would be willing to pay you more than half of his savings – sometimes even his entire savings – if you can teach him how to get a girlfriend.'

When I catch up with Tango he is in the city of Lijiang, where he's visiting his grandmother. He's also there for business. According to Tango, and others, Lijiang is China's ultimate city of love, or at least lust. Set in the heart of China's south-western Yunnan Province, Lijiang is China out of a storybook. It's small and quaint, with a skyline made up of curved rooftops instead of skyscrapers. Unlike the angular streets that have come to define much of modern Communist China, Lijiang's roads wind around in a circle, laced with traditional houses that open out into courtyards. Given the architecture – and the beautiful natural landscape that surrounds Lijiang – people have flocked here for years, either in love or looking for it.

This has proven both a blessing and a curse. Recently it has become a hotspot for wedding photos. Against any backdrop deemed beautiful, brides and grooms in wedding attire (usually Western) can be seen perched, photographer at the ready. There is no notion in China that seeing the bride in her dress before the big day is unlucky. Instead, couples believe that it is a shame to spend a large amount on an outfit that will only be worn once and sit in a wardrobe collecting dust for the rest of its life. The photos also form part of the modern-day wedding traditions, distributed to friends and relatives for the walls of their homes. And so all across China, an industry has emerged which caters to couples who wish to take nuptial photos.

Camera-shy couples are attracted to Lijiang too, walking the quaint streets arm-in-arm. Then there are the third and fourth groups of people: those looking for love and the hordes of tourists who have heard about Lijiang's picturesque reputation. They all fill the streets, turning the idyllic into an amusement park. During the holiday seasons, Lijiang is very much a good-time town, full of bars and drunk college kids. Young people go there to party and meet new people. It's like Cancun with a Chinese playlist.

For these reasons, Lijiang is the inspiration behind the name of Tango's most popular course, the Lijiang Plan. The Lijiang Plan grew out of Tango's identification that Chinese men lack 'game'. It has its origins in a blog, which Tango launched after he returned from a stint living in the US, where he familiarised himself with American dating habits. The idea was to offer an alternative dating structure to the one prevalent in China. He tells me over the phone:

> Most of the advice from parents and society is very traditional. For example, if you like a girl you should buy her flowers and dinner. You have to be generous. If you want something from her you have to give something to her. But in real life attraction is not a choice. You have to connect on other levels.

For Tango it's not what you earn or buy that counts; rather it's how you look and what you say. The emphasis on the material is doing men a disservice.

> Guys think that if a girl doesn't like them it's because they don't have the right material requirements, and so to solve the problem they believe they need to work harder and earn more. Making them feel worse is information circulating reminding them that there are more men in China.

Tango adds, 'The biggest problem is that they incorrectly present themselves at the beginning. They like to brag and lay their cards out on the table like it's a job interview. Even if someone has the goods, this tactic rarely works.'

Tango has a point. There are women who are rushing into marriage with the wrong matches out of fear of the leftover label. Equally there are those who are being choosey. As one girl said to me when I asked her whether she would rather sit in the back of a BMW crying or on a bicycle laughing, 'Neither. I want to sit in the back of a BMW laughing.'

Tango's advice – namely, first impressions should not always involve simply flashing wealth around – has struck a chord. *Southern Weekly*, a popular newspaper from China's south known for scandals mostly involving too much honest reporting, interviewed Tango and overnight he became a star.

Tango's company quickly grew from a website into a series of seminars run in major cities throughout China. At the seminars, Tango offers men step-by-step guidance ranging from their sartorial choices to dating chat. He is adamant that Chinese men do not care enough about how they look and dress, which is unfair to Chinese women, who face intense pressure to present themselves well.

Tango is keen to assert that his company is not about giving men the tools to enable them to sleep with more women. His services differ from the US 'game', which markets itself as a manual for players, a sort of antithesis of marriage. Chinese people are still more formal in the way they date and so Tango's version is used as a facilitator of marriage. Most of the people who attend his classes are not looking for more notches on the bedpost; they are looking for a wife.

His clients are predominantly wealthy, which is hardly a surprise given the course price tag – around 18,000 yuan (approximately £1,800) for the week, some four times higher than the average monthly wage in Beijing. Like those who use expensive matchmaking services, these are the men most at a loss about where they are going wrong, misled by the messages churned out by the press about women wanting rich, successful men.

Most are also well-educated, which comes as no surprise to Tango. 'They're nerds and geeks,' he says. 'Most of my Beijing clients are from the top universities like Tsinghua. For many people who attended these colleges, they had to work very hard to get there and to stay there. Their interpersonal skills aren't always great as a result.'

By way of illustration, Tango narrates the tale of one recent client. The man, who consulted Tango aged 28, attended a good college and later established a very successful publishing company, turning him into a millionaire overnight. He was struggling with romance and consulted Tango after another failed liaison. He had recently taken a woman on a first date and bought her an iPhone as a gift, which he presented at the start of the night. The date took place at a top hotel in Beijing, where he treated her to a taster meal at its flagship restaurant, ordering the most expensive foreign wines to accompany each course. The bill came to a staggering 20,000 yuan (£2,000). The next day he sent her roses to her work. She was, naturally, overwhelmed and turned down future invitations. 'I like this girl. I want to give her everything,' he told Tango as explanation. Tango says, 'I asked him, if she did the same, how would you feel?'

Tango set to work, both on his client's behaviour and on his look. He was a regular guy, neither ugly nor a heart throb, but was failing to make the best of himself. After Tango's makeover, he went speed dating, where he met a woman. This was two years ago. They later got married.

These anecdotes of success are enough to ensure Tango has a steady stream of clients; they are not enough to ensure universal approval. Older people, in particular, are critical. 'In China most people think the idea goes against that of harmony. If you use skills then people believe you are not being sincere, real or authentic. But skills help us increase our chances of meeting someone,' he says.

The idea of harmony is very ingrained in Chinese culture, stretching much further back than China's former president, Hu Jintao, who openly referenced it. It's different to the Western concept, which entails a lack of conflict. The Chinese concept is based around yin and yang, which are opposing yet necessary forces to maintain order in the universe. The two complement each other and their balance is necessary; if yin becomes stronger, yang must be weaker and vice versa. Females are yin and males are yang and it is essential to ensure the interaction between these two forces is not changed too much for fear of disrupting balance (or harmony). That Chinese people still apply these rules to dating shows how traditional values are still applicable, albeit modified, in modern China.

Tango does not believe, though, that his lessons will disrupt harmony. 'There are so many singles and the problems don't just lie with meeting new people. Chinese men also struggle with how to communicate well when they do have the chance to meet.'

IN THE MOOD FOR LOVE

Jiang, who is one of Tango's recent students, is certainly feeling positive about his experience of the Lijiang Plan. We meet one Sunday evening at a café in central Beijing. When I arrive he is slouched over the table, fast asleep. The Chinese ability to nap in the most inappropriate settings, including the office where some even have foldout beds, is something that still has the ability to surprise. I call his phone to wake him up.

Jiang is 30 years old, from Hubei Province in central China. Unlike his phone manner, which is chirpy and confident, in real life he seems cold and deadpan. Within five minutes of meeting, he looks me deep in the eyes and tells me how disenchanted he feels with Beijing, and China in general. The air and the traffic upset him, a typical complaint in Beijing. His other complaints are more unusual, at least to be spoken out loud to a complete stranger. Jiang is angered by the government and the way business works, which he thinks is controlled by too few people at the top (this, to be fair, is being articulated more openly under Xi Jinping's anti-corruption campaign). He has plans to leave China; he just doesn't know where to or when.

'I am concerned about my own personal security. Now we have Weibo and the government can get lots of information about you because of it. Two guys are in jail because of being famous and so people started to dig into their past. Being famous is not that good, nor is being wealthy.' Here Jiang presents the flipside of the internet's power to expand horizons.

He recently started working as a designer for a games company specialising in role-play games. The company's customers (usually men in their twenties and thirties) spend huge amounts of cash on props in the game. Industry is booming. The country's trade group GPC tracked industry revenues for 2013 at 83.17 billion Chinese yuan (£8.82 billion), up 38 per cent from the previous year, with predictions that China would overtake the US as world number one for mobile games by the close of 2014. The amount of money staying in China is also growing. In 2013, domestically developed games brought in more than 57.3 per cent of the country's gaming revenues.

It's good news for Jiang. The company which he works for is riding the wave of gaming's success, being already worth 2 billion yuan and bestowing its employees with decent monthly salaries.

Jiang is less successful romantically. He has been single all of his life, save for one six-month relationship. As the curtain closed on his twenties, Jiang grew tired of his solo status and sought the help of Tango after spotting his ad online. It was time to take control, in life and in love.

'It's about generally how to get along with everyone, how to be a team leader. I want to be an alpha male,' he says in a very serious tone, holding my gaze for a few seconds.

'I could talk to girls as friends, but never as a boyfriend and I wanted to find a girlfriend. I was always called the "nice guy" on a date. I was sensitive and would buy the girls gifts.' As Jiang tells me about this I am reminded of all of the jokes that are circulating about Chinese men being emasculated by girls. China is still a man's world, but it is fairly commonplace for young wannabe Romeos to shower girls in attention and gifts in an incredibly doting fashion. Seeing couples in matching outfits is common too, as are men carrying their girlfriends' handbags.

I ask Jiang what gifts he bought for the girls he took on dates.

'Anything really. If we walked past a store and they liked stuff in the window, I would buy it for them.'

Like the other clients of Tango, the first part of the course concentrated on improving Jiang's image.

'He taught me how to dress like a gentleman. Before I was an IT nerd. No girl wants an IT nerd,' he laments. For our coffee date, Jiang is wearing jeans (new), a turquoise polo shirt (new) and simple framed glasses (old). His face has been given an edge by carefully crafted facial hair, which he believes makes him look more masculine – an interesting Western affectation (even today Chinese masculinity is less tied to muscles and body hair and more to intellect first and being a martial arts warrior second, as plenty of movies from Chinese and Hong Kong cinema attest. So-called studs in the Chinese celebrity sphere are often very groomed and immaculate in their appearance, control being a central tenet, in direct contrast to Western takes on masculinity).

The second part of the course was supposedly to instil in him confidence in any given situation. Here was the real struggle, something which he believed united him with his fellow countrymen. They are good at hanging out with men, far less so with women.

Perhaps for some Chinese men this is the result of the One Child Policy denying them the neutralising presence of a potentially female sibling, or at least company of a similar age. Anthropologists and behavioural psychologists have debated this very topic. That the policy has led to a generation of socially awkward kids is one theory proposed, with some persuasive data to back it up. Yet, as mentioned in more depth earlier, some demographers calculate that as many as two-thirds of China's population were not bound by the One Child Policy from its inception in 1979 to its significant amendment in 2013, meaning links between the character of Chinese youth and lack of siblings are weak.

The course adopts a pragmatic approach. Jiang was taught an array of tactics which enabled him to grow in confidence and seize opportunities in all walks of life. After the course he met plenty more women than before. Most significantly, his present girlfriend.

Their meeting was totally out of Tango's playbook. Jiang was walking down the popular tourist and shopping area of Wanfujing when he saw a girl that he liked the look of. Trained by the course, he positioned himself in front of her and just to the side, rather than trailing behind – the perfect position to spark up a conversation. They got chatting, exchanged numbers and went on a date (to McDonald's, no less). She was 23 years old, a 1990s kid, which in China makes her a different generation – *jiulinghou*, as they are called, meaning post-1990s generation. *Jiulinghou* are believed to be even more materialistic than their immediate seniors. Two common jokes in China sum up nicely how people perceive – and in turn pigeonhole – these youngsters. The first, on the note of attitude to work, goes: those born in the 1970s work all the time, those born in the 1980s refuse to work overtime, those born in the 1990s refuse to work at all. The second homes in on spending habits: 1970s kids save their money, 1980s kids spend their money, 1990s kids spend their parents' money.

'The 1990s kids care more about themselves. Us 1980s kids care more about others,' Jiang tells me. Nevertheless, they got on well and, again trained by the course, he waited until recently before buying her gifts, he tells me proudly. With that he salutes to the waitress, pays the bill and swaggers off to meet his girlfriend for a cinema date, posturing in a way that is every bit the alpha male.

What is interesting about the new, successful middle class, and both Huang and Jiang are examples of this, is that they're no longer content to have just their material needs met. Their attitudes are typical of many young urban Chinese, whose slogan could well be 'To fall in love is glorious', not just 'To get rich is glorious'. These young men and women are balancing pragmatism with romance in order to cope with a new culture based on market principles. This helps explain why the results are often contradictory and why Chinese youth cannot be easily pigeonholed. These contradictions are arguably most acute in the modern Chinese craze for big, brash 'Western' weddings, which will now be addressed.

4

Red Wedding
Capitalism Meets Communism in Chinese Marriage

Parents might look at a simple, elegant flower arrangement and say it's not enough, that it doesn't look like [they've] spent enough.
Miyoshi, a wedding planner in Beijing

Given the pressure to get married that touches everyone in China, it's no surprise that weddings are a big deal. Each year 10 million couples get married in China, and their nuptials are very important events. They are seen as a key passage in adulthood and a time for the family to show itself off to the world. Their current manifestation also shows the different sides of modern China, fusing traditional Chinese rituals with modern traditions inspired by popular culture from both East and West.

Take Lili's wedding as an example. She's a 26-year-old girl who wears androgynous clothing and is the opposite of a 'girly' girl. She has a lot of attitude and likes to poke fun at the establishment. And yet within a year she will be transformed. At various locations throughout Beijing Lili will strike a pose in front of a camera wearing a selection of meringue dresses and looking every bit like a modern-day princess.

As mentioned earlier, wedding photos are now an integral part of courtship in the country. Young Chinese couples often have a series of photos taken in their wedding outfits at scenic spots or in a studio with a nice backdrop before, during and after the wedding. Some couples – often the super-rich – even travel abroad to take the photos.

Lili is pretty excited by this stage and already planning her own photos for when she feels 'slim enough'. She says,

One of my friends, who got married last year, is going to take photos around Beijing. She has five dresses. She is going to take 120 photos and then pick 15 to 20 of them. One of the locations for the photos is inside a nice garden. It will cost around 5,000 yuan [£500] for those things, which is really cheap. Most of my friends take photos for 8,000 to 10,000 yuan. They will put the photos in an album and have one on the wall of their bedroom.

I have read and seen enough brides around China to know that the photos are pretty ubiquitous. I had even done a shoot myself, one day with a friend in Shanghai for fun. It is easy enough to find a photo studio in most areas of any major city and they come stocked with plenty of wedding dresses, in case you don't have your own. What I am curious about is just how prolific the photos are. Does everyone take them or is that just my impression from having seen so many?

'Yes. Everyone does the photos,' Lili answers with conviction. 'Or at least all of my friends, and we are fairly ordinary.'

At present there's no sign Lili's engaged: she keeps her ring hidden under lock and key, only making outings on special occasions. Wedding bands are a Western import that have taken off in China in recent years. Some are starting to spend big on a ring; plenty more do not have one at all, or at the least do not wear theirs regularly.

'I don't want to make people jealous. Some of the girls at work, they are a little older and still single. They will be so jealous,' says Lili. 'Some of us don't have a ceremony because we want to save money, or we will just treat a few people,' she adds, on the particulars of the wedding itself. Lili always assumed she would have a big party, though, and there's no way her parents would allow anything else.

'Of course I will have a ceremony. I'm so popular! There are many people to invite!' She isn't being modest here, and rightly so. Lili's charisma translates into a busy social schedule. Next year the couple will get their wedding certificate. The year after they will have the wedding party at a very popular local restaurant. In between getting the certificate and the party they will continue to live separately, which she claims is a fairly standard state of affairs. Other details concerning the wedding are being fine-tuned at present.

As Lili's example shows, modern Chinese weddings are an intriguing melange of different traditions, some familiar, some not at all. They have arrived at this point as a result of a complex evolution over the past 100 years.

I have been fascinated by Chinese weddings for some time, particularly since viewing the film *Red Sorghum*, Zhang Yimou's directorial debut from the 1980s. The opening scene is the film's most evocative. It features 'My grandmother', as the character is known, a young Chinese girl being carried through dusty fields of sorghum in a red sedan on her wedding day. Her couriers bellow songs about how unfortunate the man is she is set to marry, while she cries inside. One of her carriers is called 'My grandfather', and it quickly becomes clear that she is attracted to him and he to her. She later goes on to lose her virginity to the carrier, not her husband, in a scene that marked a break from China's past. Not long after this scene, her husband passes away under dubious circumstances and 'My grandmother' is able to unite with the sedan carrier for good.

The film represented a junction in China. While it was set in 1930s China, it was symbolic of the country's crossroads at the end of the 1980s. China's social changes were in their infancy. Free choice in the marriage market was granted, albeit within a context.

The film's greater meaning aside, it presented a visually intoxicating portrait of the traditional Chinese wedding. According to traditional wedding customs, the journey in the sedan chair would have marked the middle of the rituals. Traditional weddings were based on a comprehensive system of etiquette. Different ceremonies and rituals were practised in different regions, with some of the traditions dating back thousands of years. Certain aspects became more commonplace than others. It's possible to talk in slightly more generalised terms of what a wedding might have looked like across a large time and place, so long as the reader bears in mind that there would have been nuances in different times and different regions.

Traditional weddings in China emphasised the transfer of a girl from her birth family to her future husband's. The process began with an elaborate marriage proposal and acceptance. For the most part this was about making sure the two families were a good match for harmony, with many third parties being involved. At the same time, superstition was key. For example, if the bride's family were happy to go ahead with the wedding plans, they would present the girl's birth certificate to the groom's family, who would place this document on the ancestral altar for three days. If no inauspicious omens occurred, such as quarrels between concerned parties, the parents would give the information to an astrological expert to confirm the pair were a good match.

Assuming the outcome was favourable, the next stage was preparation for the wedding. A dowry was presented to the bride's side, a present in exchange for their daughter. Invitations were sent out in red envelopes. Sometimes snacks gifted to the bride's family by the groom were redistributed to their friends and relatives as part of this invite.

Next came the wedding day itself. A typical wedding ceremony would have included the bride undergoing an elaborate hairdressing and bathing ceremony to symbolise her passage into adulthood. Back at the groom's house, the wedding bed would be prepared. Children were invited onto the bed, which was covered in snacks, such as fresh fruit and nuts. Both the children and the food symbolised fertility, a marker of the marriage being about the production of family heirs.

While this was going on, the groom would kneel at a family altar and his father would place a red cap on his head. He would pray to his ancestors and parents. Then he would head over to the woman's home, arriving with great fanfare. She would board the sedan, typically crying as she left the place where she was born. Sometimes this was out of a sense of duty – if you didn't cry it meant you were a terrible daughter. Other times, of course, these were genuine tears as a girl was torn from her family and married off to a man she may not have set eyes on until that day.

The woman would then be brought to the husband's home, where the ceremony would commence. The procession was accompanied by a very noisy orchestra and an abundance of firecrackers. Once the bride was at her new home, the ceremony required the couple to bow before every member of the man's family. A huge meal followed, hosted by the man's family to celebrate the new relationship. Games were played, often suggestive in nature. For example, a common game involved the bride moving an egg up one leg and down the other. After the feast the couple would go to their wedding chamber and consummate the marriage, signalling the end of the nuptials.

The weddings were bright, festive, loud and inebriated affairs. Red – representing happiness, power and luck in China – was the dominant colour. On top of the invitations, the bride and groom's clothes were red, the sedan chair was red and the decorations and other embellishments were red.

These traditions came to a halt with the Communist Revolution of 1949, when weddings underwent a severe facelift. They were still red under Mao, but Communist red rather than literally red. Most aspects of the traditional wedding did not chime with the values being exalted under Chairman Mao. They were perceived as bourgeois and did not suit a world in which women were meant to have more choice and not be treated like property passed from one house to another. Arranged marriages and concubines were banned, and 'love' marriages were promoted.

This was the theory, at least. The reality was different. A whole set of other conventions ensured that choice was still far from free. Under the early Communists, a saying came to dominate: 'Personal matters, even the biggest, are still small;

political matters, even the smallest, are still big.' Within the context of class struggle, matches had to be between parties of the same class background. Those whose backgrounds were considered tainted found themselves hugely disadvantaged in 'New China', while those working for the Chinese state enjoyed unprecedented popularity in the marriage market. They were deemed ideologically sound and in a stable, well-paid profession. Even then, marrying into a 'high' class involved other hurdles, which again made it less about free choice. For example, before a military officer could be betrothed, the prospective partner had to undergo an exam. In short, the state simply took over the role of matchmaker from people at a local level. Meanwhile, marriage and the family continued to be central to the structure of Chinese society.

That the people's energy was to be channelled into class struggle – at least superficially – translated into a vastly different wedding ceremony. The practice of giving a dowry was particularly discouraged for this reason. All the symbolism surrounding the bride moving from one family to another was replaced by a more simple ceremony marking the creation of a new unit. Gone were decorative outfits and rich colours. In came military uniforms and simple ceremonies, if there were ceremonies at all. Bowing to the family and relatives was also removed; instead couples would bow before a portrait of Chairman Mao.

Within this context, the couple's workplace bosses began to play a role in wedding ceremonies. With the *danwei* – work unit – being a major institution in a person's life under Mao, people's *laoban* – boss – took on a central role, often officiating the ceremony.

These changes were made obsolete after the opening-up from the late 1970s. A sort of cultural amnesia took over, with the Maoist period representing a void in the memory of Chinese marriage. Certain practices from the traditional wedding resurfaced. These continue to be practised to this day. At the same time, they have fused with Western wedding practices, creating a hybrid which is as much familiar as it is foreign. With Western romantic comedies now accessible and commonplace, many Chinese couples have started to follow American wedding customs. In the most obvious example, the white wedding dress has made its Chinese debut.

LOVE COMMODIFIED

The trajectory of the Chinese wedding has moved, along with wider trends in the middle class, from austerity to extravagance. Even distasteful pictures that circulated in October 2014 of a couple married in the theme of the Cultural Revolution hinted at a lavish ceremony. In Beijing, the average cost of a wedding is around 80,000 yuan (£8,000), and this sum does not include the cost of the ring, the clothes, trips and wedding-day pictures. Given the emphasis placed on the family and conformity, weddings are very important. And they also double as a way a family can show off its success. For example, a wedding in 2013 in Chongqing, Sichuan Province, became the most expensive the city had seen when the wealthy father of the groom decided to invest more in it to seize on a business opportunity.

'At first I was aiming to keep extravagance and waste to a minimum. But then I decided to combine the wedding with a corporate promotion event,' he said. '[The banquet] allows me to kill two birds with one stone [...] I feel the money has been well spent,' the father told reporters.

The parents on the groom's side typically pay for most of the wedding. If they do not have enough funds, the couple will chip in. It's not unheard of for couples to spend their entire year's salaries on the day.

Of the traditions that have survived, there is still a formal meeting of the parents, who negotiate aspects of the marriage. There is also still a dowry, now going directly to the couple as a means of helping them out. The dowry joins the stock of money the couple receive from their guests, who are expected to endow the couple with red sachets of money or even credit cards linked to new bank accounts, a growing trend in particularly affluent social circles. And, despite the Communist Party's attempts to wipe out forms of religion and superstitions, the modern Chinese wedding shows that certain beliefs have survived. The date, in particular, has to be auspicious for the wedding, determined by feng shui or astrology. A wedding can easily take place during the working week if the day is deemed good luck. For example, the number eight – *ba* – is seen as the luckiest number due to the pronunciation of the word being similar to *fa*, which means wealth and fortune (the number four – *si* – by comparison is the least lucky as it sounds like the Chinese word for death). Getting married on a date associated with the number eight is highly coveted, as was seen during the Beijing Olympic Games, when weddings were held across China on the opening day, which was on the eighth day of the eighth month in 2008.

I was invited to a Chinese wedding which took place on a Monday. A sizable minority could not make it and the couple had to be very understanding. After the wedding those who were unable to attend were given goodie bags containing sweets and chocolates, which is customary and dates back centuries. Every wedding host gives guests these sweets; it would be strange not to.

On the day of the ceremony, a Chinese bride traditionally goes into seclusion with her closest friends. As with the ceremonies of yore, immediately before departing for the wedding the groom and his best man will pick up the bride, while the bridesmaids will try, playfully, to keep them out.

The bride will either be clad in a traditional red gown or a Western white one. Sometimes she will opt for both, modelled at different times during the evening. Beijing is full of bridal shops where brides-to-be can purchase any outfit to suit their tastes. Huge meringue-style dresses adorn their windows. Glitter and sparkles, which find their way onto many articles of clothing in China, are visible. Display cases exhibit costume jewellery, with tiaras a particular trend. Gaudy is an understatement. Even platform heels glow from the number of rhinestones encrusted on them. The price tags in these stores vary from expensive to obscene. It is far removed from the days of Mao suits.

These shops are growing in number by the day, and they're wildly lucrative. In 2013 the bridal industry was estimated to be worth £38 billion by the China Wedding Industry Development Report, and as the middle class grows, so too does bridal spending. Saying 'I do' is not cheap in China.

It's not just the dress that has been upgraded. The sedan chair has now been superseded by a luxury car, usually decorated with fresh flowers. The car can be just one of many in a procession which will slowly drive through town as men throw fireworks and film the occasion. For some incredibly wealthy families Rolls Royce motorcades or brides arriving via helicopter have been known.

In stark contrast, the ceremony itself is relatively simple. In the absence of formal, structured religion, few conventions creep in. Couples might even be married in group ceremonies. The most important part is what happens after the ceremony – the banquet. Wedding banquets remain marathon events spread over many hours, or even days. In some instances, they have continued for as long as three days. Like the meal at Chinese New Year, a huge variety of dishes are served and the type of food is carefully selected. There will always be fish, as the pronunciation of the Chinese word for fish (*yu*) means abundance. There will often be chicken and lobster, which, based on ancient symbolism, signifies a good balance of yin and yang. During the course of the banquet, the bride is also expected to change outfits, as a sign of her wealth and status. Finally, Chinese wedding banquets are notoriously liquor-laden. The groom typically circulates the tables taking shots of alcohol at each stop. Best men are sometimes chosen for their ability to keep apace, or even step in and drink when the groom has reached his limit.

As implied, another element has recently come to characterise the Chinese wedding, a 'Western' affectation – showbiz. Chinese couples want to be the star of their own show. The rapid growth in Chinese wedding magazines and bridal websites has refined tastes and stoked desires. Hollywood chick flicks add to this. Popular wedding trends that I have heard of are renting misting machines, a staple of music and fashion videos, to provide a romantic atmosphere, and paying exorbitant fees for famous singers to act as the entertainment. To Western readers these anecdotes seem similar to the lavish celebrity nuptials we have become accustomed to. The major difference lies in their newness; while we watched *Father of the Bride* as kids, Chinese children were watching *Red Sorghum*, if they saw any movie featuring weddings at all. The weddings of twenty-first-century China once again show how fast the country is moving and how an older generation has been left behind.

CHINESE WEDDING PLANNERS: MAKING MONEY OUT OF MARRIAGE

The evolution of the Chinese wedding ceremony has been good news for China's entrepreneurs and many are taking a slice of the new market. Wedding planners are the latest to get in on the act. Miyoshi Nakahara, a half-Japanese, half-Taiwanese woman, owns and runs an eponymous wedding-planning company. It is now one of the country's top such companies and is often featured in Chinese *Vogue* and other glossy magazines.

I meet Miyoshi to discuss the industry in more detail. It's a miserable Monday afternoon, and like many places in Beijing, her studio is not easy to find. It is in an apartment complex tucked behind a main road in the Central Business District of Beijing, presumably located to accommodate people who want to make appointments during their lunch hour. Away from the noise of the busy thoroughfare, Miyoshi's office is bright and airy, a series of interlinking rooms dedicated to different aspects of a wedding service. A handful of creative staff mill around the studio. One room doubles as a florist's.

Miyoshi, slight in frame and with a delicate, pretty face, is excited when I meet her. She is soon to get married herself in a wedding that will take place at Maison Boulud, one of the city's best restaurants. After a tour of the studio, we sit down and discuss her business. Miyoshi started her company three years ago, after spending two years at another wedding company and attending a wedding training course just before that. In order to do this course, she had to return to Japan briefly; back in 2008, wedding-planning courses were not available in Beijing. Now Beijing offers three such courses – a sign of how fast the industry is growing.

The wedding company she worked for before founding her own was not her style. At the time wedding companies in China would offer packages. Clients would choose a package based on budget and that, alongside the date, was where their decisions began and ended. After the choice was made, the company would take care of everything else, using exactly the same flowers, photographer and so on within the package, creating replica weddings according to price. It wasn't for Miyoshi.

'I wanted to do something whereby I could get to know the couples more and incorporate their personalities in the events. I didn't feel like I was a wedding planner, just a sales person,' she explains.

When Miyoshi was at her old company she started to organise the weddings of some expats in Beijing, which was where her ambitions saw fruit.

'They wanted unique flowers and more details,' she says, adding that this allowed her to move away from the package deals. Her clients responded well, as did people in Beijing at large. With few companies offering bespoke weddings at the time, Miyoshi's approach landed her company in the glossy pages of *Cosmopolitan*, amongst other magazines. As she tells me this, she grabs the iPad that has been sitting on the table between us, displaying a carousel of pretty bridal images. She shows me a slideshow of one of her past weddings; the nuptials of a Jewish and Catholic couple who used modern embellishments in a traditional Chinese setting.

'All the locals were like, "Oh, you can have weddings like this?!"'

On the success of this and other endeavours, Miyoshi broke free and set up her own company. Miyoshi now has an even split of Chinese and foreign clients. Initially there was an exchange; a lot of foreigners wanted to do traditional Chinese weddings, while many Chinese liked a Western one. After a while, more Chinese people started going back to their old roots. For example, she recently did the wedding of a Chinese couple in which the bride arrived in a red sedan, surrounded by actors dressed in costume pretending to be traditional servers. It was Qing Dynasty style, known for its loud and happy nuptials. Apparently, different dynasties came to be known for their distinct styles. The iPad comes out again. Approximately a dozen rosy-cheeked men clad in red smile around a coy-looking bride. It looks like Disney's *Mulan* in reality.

Miyoshi's company sits at the highest end. She has done three weddings this year costing over 1 million yuan (£100,000), two of which were for Chinese couples. The ascent of the million-dollar wedding in China reflects that the Chinese have more cash to spend. It is also an enactment of another form of social etiquette.

'Many people in China spend a lot on weddings. They see it as a big deal and Chinese people need to save face, so parents will spend big.' And sometimes it is not just the parents who see the occasion as a social marker. One of Miyoshi's friend's husbands comes from an impoverished background and has become very rich in real estate. His wedding was an important occasion to show off his new status. Four hundred people attended an event that was extravagant even by Miyoshi's standards. A sea of exquisite flowers filled the room and LCD screens broadcast pictures of the couple and the man on the walls.

'He had his face and his parents were really proud of him,' Miyoshi says of the event.

Proposals have taken on Chinese characteristics too. As a Western import, when the ring first started shining in China, it was integrated into the ceremony. Brides would be proposed to by their grooms on the aisle. As exposure to Western romcoms has increased, brides-to-be now expect a ring in advance.

Engagements are often done in public. Photographers are hired; colleagues and friends gather around as the proposal has become a party in itself.

These changes are good news for Miyoshi. As the wedding-planning industry grows, it evolves into a much more established, well-managed affair. Until recently, wedding planners were not well-educated. The idea of a professional photographer was not contemplated; hacks with cameras would normally act the part. Now university graduates want to join companies such as hers.

Miyoshi sounds as if she is living the Chinese dream. There's scope to make lots of money and room to be creative in a relatively young industry. It's the sort of occupation that attracts people from all corners of the globe to come to China. It is perceived as the land of opportunity, the place to get rich quick. This is especially the case in Asia. Expats I have spoken to from countries such as Malaysia say that only ten years ago they would have considered London and New York as ideal destinations for their career. Now they look to Shanghai and Beijing. However, like the US of the nineteenth century, there is still a Wild West character to the country. The energy is intoxicating, but daily life can be full of frustrations and challenges. The serene offices of Miyoshi Nakahara are not immune.

'In China people look down on the wedding industry. My clients don't say much, but their parents will think, "Oh, wedding companies charge lots and we can't trust them,"' Miyoshi tells me of how the past poor reputation continues to blight the industry.

'Before, there were a lot of unethical people who would just take your money. They would even show fake weddings. Some companies stole my own photos and put them on their website saying they could deliver this and of course at a fraction of the cost!' Miyoshi explains this in a way that suggests she finds it as much funny and silly as it is annoying.

The generation gap is a constant friction when working with clients. Miyoshi often encounters a discrepancy between what parents want and what their offspring want, having been exposed to completely different media and pressures growing up. The idea of personalised weddings has been met with resistance as she battles the forces of tradition and pushy elders. For example, a local Beijing tradition is to hold a wedding before midday. Otherwise it is seen as embarrassing; post-lunch weddings are the preserve of second marriages. Different cities have different rules. In Tianjin, which is only a short train journey away, couples traditionally get married at night.

Many Beijing couples that she meets have yet to shrug off the tradition as their parents insist on it. The formula of the morning wedding is less than ideal. The bride has to fight off falling asleep, having risen around five to do her hair, make-up and other rituals.

Then there is the matter of differing tastes between the generations: 'The young go for design and style, while the parents might look at a simple, elegant flower arrangement and say it's not enough, that it doesn't look like [they've] spent enough.'

As I go to leave the studio, Miyoshi points to a framed certificate dangling from the wall. It is from 2012 and announces third prize in the first Table Setting and Centrepieces Contest for her company.

'It was very important for China and for the industry here,' she says, the pride in her eyes like a parent's in front of their child's school portrait. She caresses the side of the frame as I make my exit.

Miyoshi and other wedding planners show how Chinese youth are increasingly able to dictate their own lives, down to their weddings, which until recently were affairs in the hands of parents, professional matchmakers or even company bosses.

On top of having more choice on who to wed, having more say in how they wed is a freedom which is an important change for Chinese youth. At the same time, the evolution of the wedding industry shows how intimate and personal relations have become more explicitly commodified and linked to global processes. With that they present new opportunities – and new challenges. The generation gap widens further, as does the divide between the nation's haves and have-nots.

For some people, the commodification of love has become so extreme that they are willing to sacrifice the emotional support of a loving relationship and to turn their personal lives into more professional arrangements. We will meet these people in the next chapter.

5

The Other Woman
Mistress Culture

*He said in a very deadpan way, 'I can't. I have a wife
and kid.' I was in bed. My heart sank. I was really in
love at the time.*
Mei, on dating a married man

One of the less-talked-about but equally ubiquitous sides
of love in China is that of the mistress. Keeping another
woman is in the country's historical fabric. Emperors came with
a harem of concubines, as the country's most famous classic and
raunchy novel narrates. *Dream of the Red Chamber* outlines the
story of an imperial concubine in the Qing Dynasty who supports her entire family, including its own numerous concubines,
thanks to the Emperor's patronage. Outside the imperial palace,
Chinese men were often married to more than one woman, each
of whom would have been kept in their own households.

Monogamy only arrived in China in the 1950s, when
marriage laws banned the keeping of other wives. Even then
many broke the law. Chairman Mao himself had a soft spot for
women who were not his wife.

In the China of today, the tradition of keeping a mistress
has not only survived, it has flourished. It is particularly
common amongst powerful Chinese men. A study by the Crisis
Management Centre at Renmin University in Beijing, published
at the start of 2013, showed that 95 per cent of corrupt officials
had illicit affairs and 60 per cent of them had kept a mistress.
It's actually illegal for a government official to keep a mistress
and yet these numbers mark an increase on those from only a
few years earlier. According to a government report in 2007,

90 per cent of top officials brought down by corruption scandals had kept a mistress – and in many cases they had more than one. Former Railways Minister Liu Zhijun, who was jailed for corruption, reportedly kept 18.

Another case that has dominated newspaper headlines is that of Ji Yingnan. She shamed her former lover in the full glare of China's millions of microblog users when she posted videos and pictures of the two of them online. These included the pair enjoying shopping sprees, splashing about in a private swimming pool and at a party where the official asked his mistress to marry him. The 26-year-old identified her lover as Fan Yue, a deputy director at the State Administration of Archives. Ji claimed she exposed him after discovering he was married with a teenage son. She hadn't realised he had lied to her and thought that one day she would actually marry him. What particularly shocked the public were the staggering sums of cash involved. According to Ji, Fan gave her more than $1,000 (£650) a day in pocket money on top of buying her a luxury car.

That infidelity is rife within China is hardly a surprise. As already shown, many people enter marriages after dating for only a short time as a result of pressure from parents, which can spell trouble. China is also still a society dominated by men, and as we have seen love and materialism are intertwined. The exploitation of young women by powerful men is an inevitable result. This is not helped by the current vast chasm between the rich and the poor. Given a historical context which perpetuates the notion that having a mistress equals having status and power, mistresses remain a status symbol for those at the top. Li Yinhe, a prominent sexologist in China, once stated that many Chinese men believe they are still living in imperial times: 'I think many Chinese men have an emperor's complex. Being an emperor means you can have many women. This is something they are proud of. They see women as trophies of their success.'

Echoing Li's argument is Zheng Tiantian, author of the book *Red Lights: The Lives of Sex Workers in Postsocialist China*. As part of research for her book, Zheng spent several years posing as a hostess at three different establishments in the northern city of Dalian to get under the skin of China's sex industry. Hostesses are different from prostitutes in that they do not always have sex with clients. Instead they are there to flatter the clients' egos and provide entertainment, which sometimes includes intercourse. Most of the clients who visit the young girls are middle-aged men and some of these girls go on to become their mistresses.

I spoke to Zheng about whether visiting KTV girls, those who work at the vast network of karaoke joints across China which are known to offer far more than a friendly singalong, is more stigmatised amongst the post-1980s generation compared to earlier generations. Are these habits that China's youth will pick up and perpetuate? Zheng believes age does not make a difference. 'As far as I know, it is never stigmatised,' she tells me firmly. The reason the men are older is less to do with attitude and more to do with economics. The requisite tip for a hostess is not cheap, nor is keeping a mistress; the habit has become a staple of the business world. Zheng adds: 'Consumption of women is a basis for men to evaluate each other's traits and characteristics and select business partners in their alliance.'

Herein lies a key point: that high-powered professional men have affairs is not uncommon anywhere in the world. The fundamental difference is that elsewhere an affair is usually a secret, whereas Chinese men openly support such behaviour as a way of distinguishing wealth and social standing. It's basically an open secret: an entire culture of Mad Men who are not confined to the 1960s or to the TV screen. China's sex ratio imbalance exacerbates this. With fewer women in the population, young, available ones are perceived as a rare commodity.

Zheng's study is limited to women who work directly in the sex industry. These women are predominantly uneducated, poor and from the countryside. They pick up sex work at the karaoke bars, massage parlours and nightclubs and their approach is rooted in pragmatism, as they use sex as a means to better their lives. Many of the young women send money home to families, often keeping their occupation secret from them.

It is a different story for urban, educated women who end up as mistresses. They get into these sorts of relationships just as much through chance as through choice. Some begin innocently, through a genuine sense of attraction and unaware of their lover's marital status, as was the case of Ji Yingnan mentioned above. Others are less naive or even openly choose mistress as a status.

A term has arisen to describe women who are official mistresses – *ernai* or 'second wife'. The *ernai* are usually paid a salary and some are provided accommodation. Those who are mistresses as their day job might demand housing near other mistresses and there are now entire neighbourhoods in China's first-tier cities known as *ernaicun*, literally 'mistress villages'. These areas house beauty salons, massage parlours, shops and restaurants. For estate agents it's been a blessing in disguise. The mistress culture is solving a central problem of real estate in China – how to deal with all those empty apartments built at the height of China's property boom.

In exchange for money and property the women offer sex and company when needed. Romance is not expected; neither are children, though a degree of exclusivity is. Details are sometimes laid out in contracts in advance. But there are ways to circumvent these contracts. I recently heard of a woman who is a mistress to three men, all of whom believe they are her only partner. She asks each of them for the same expensive gifts. Once they have delivered, she sells two of the three and keeps the final one, which she uses around all three, who do not suspect it is a different one to their gift. This woman's story shows the extent of agency some women have in these relationships. It's not simply a case of men deceiving women in modern China.

For those who become mistresses as early as in college, it is about contacts as much as it is money. Richard Burger in *Behind the Red Door: Sex in China* quotes one netizen outlining the difference between first wives, second wives and prostitutes:

Prostitutes are a bit like a paid public toilet, they're there to fulfill a basic need and anyone who has the money can use them. An *ernai* is like a private toilet – you need to be fairly well off to have one, no one else can use it, and you take much better care of it than a public toilet. And a wife? Well, you wouldn't want to compare her to any kind of toilet at all, because she is your equal.

An *ernai* agency operates in Shanghai, providing a menu of potential college students for men willing to pay. The annual maintenance fees range from approximately £2,000 for students from less renowned campuses to around £17,000 for those from the elite. The girls who partake in these extracurricular activities are not exceptions. So prolific is the practice that Chongqing Normal University in Sichuan Province and South China Normal University in Guangzhou both instituted rules to expel girls involved in the industry. Guangzhou, in the province of Guangdong, also passed legislation in 2007 that outlawed the keeping of mistresses. Upon failure to enforce it, the same province introduced classes in elementary and high schools to try to address the issue. Young girls were taught a new subject: how to avoid becoming a mistress. The provincial government's solution was a pioneering 'female education programme' which taught girls to depend on themselves for their future, as opposed to relying on a man.

In certain instances *ernai* graduate into *xiao san* – a third party – those who have fallen in love with the man and wish for him to leave his wife. Such was the case in 2013 when a video went viral showing a pregnant woman turning up to the wedding of her lover and starting a blazing fight between herself and the bride.

'*Xiao san* expect to marry the man because they've invested so much: their youth and their love,' explains San Jie, a 22-year-old founder of a website for *xiao san*, as told in Burger's book. Her website, the China Association for the Care of Xiao San, was launched in 2007 in order to lessen the pain and frustration she observed amongst her friends, who were all *xiao san*. It has 500 members and a joining fee of 100 yuan (£10). Frequently asked questions on the site include ones on whether their man really loves them.

It is not just about money or contacts. Genuine love and affection do exist in some instances. Moreover, it is not just men who cheat. There are examples of wives having extramarital liaisons too, albeit in a far less institutionalised way.

LEARNING THE TRICKS OF THE MISTRESS TRADE

Mei is more than happy to remain an *ernai* and not become a *xiao san*, although happy might be the wrong word – her experience with men's unfaithfulness is not a source of contentment, as she outlines to me:

> One day we [her then boyfriend and herself] were talking about hypothetical dreams, such as moving to New York. I suggested we both sell our places and leave the city. He said in a very deadpan way, 'I can't. I have a wife and kid.' I was in bed. My heart sank. I was really in love at the time.

Mei narrates her story to me over lunch. We are just around the corner from her work, on the ground floor of a high-end hotel, one that no doubt thrives on the culture of infidelity. An hour earlier Mei had come breezing through its swing doors, a confident spring in her step. She is pretty, petite and very well put together. Her voice matches her appearance, soft and delicate. She appears in control. She had quickly directed me past the lobby to a new salad bar in the hotel. It is full of corporate clientele. Rows of people in suits sit with their laptops on the table, clicking and eating. As she tells me her story, she lowers her voice a few decibels. Her confidence seems to evaporate with it.

Mei lives in an exclusive apartment complex in a nice, leafy area of town. It was there that she met the man. He was 31 years old and they kept sharing a lift together. He was a nice-looking man, albeit one who had a bit of a belly, a look which in China still implies a life free from want. On one lift ride he asked her out for lunch and that quickly led to them sleeping together.

The relationship was convenient and he took good care of her. I ask exactly what that entailed. Gifts, she responds. Nice handbags, and nice dinners too. Not to mention compliments. The general trappings of someone who cared. He was also funny and smart. It was all going well, until he casually told her he had a wife and child.

Mei tried to break it off, but due to loneliness and, by that stage, love, she relapsed several times. All the while her curiosity got the better of her. She started to fish around for more details on his matrimonial life. It turned out that he was the doting father of a two-year-old, with a gorgeous wife whom he loved but was not necessarily in love with (according to him). The wife and child lived in the southern island Hainan, where he spent half of his time. She was an estate agent who had shown him a house when he was looking to invest in property down there and she got pregnant before they were married, which led to their marriage. He was a wealthy businessman with ties to the government – Mei is reluctant to reveal more than this. In Mei's case, he actually offered to divorce his wife. Mei declined. 'I didn't want him to divorce her. I didn't want all of the baggage,' she responded to my questioning.

This is not Mei's first experience of infidelity. Several years earlier she had been the one cheated on, so she knows what it feels like. In fact, Mei's experience of infidelity is almost synonymous with her experience of men.

She is from Hunan Province, the province known for its spicy food and as the birthplace of Chairman Mao. Her mother is a doctor and her father a government official. It's a good background for a fourth-tier city and allowed for a degree of comfort while growing up, within a context. The family could support themselves and were not working on a farm – nothing more, nothing less. Her relatives, on the other hand, are all farmers on an average household income of 10,000 yuan (£1,000) a month and under. As a result, her parents are held up as the shining examples in both families, the only ones who went to university. It is Mei's perception of her childhood as fragile that has affected her views now. This hangover from the past affects many of today's youth, who grow up insecure about how long their newfound wealth will last.

When growing up Mei was very close to her father's side, where she played the role of big sister to her two cousins. She was particularly helpful when it came to their schooling. Mei was top of her class and wanted to assist them in achieving similar results.

'However, they weren't very good academically. I was working hard to teach them in order to better their situation,' she says.

To this day, Mei continues to help out her cousins and her aunt, supporting them financially by sending home some of her pay cheque every month. It's a pretty common situation. Many Chinese youth send home money to less-well-off relatives and one wonders whether the pressure to not only support yourself but also your family in a wider sense is fuelling some of these less desirable sexual situations.

'I have a very close relationship with my aunt. She acted like my *nani* [grandmother] and supported me when my parents couldn't afford it,' she says, as if she needed to justify her actions.

On sleeping with older, wealthier men, Mei is very honest and unapologetic in her reasoning: 'It's very hard finding love in Beijing. If you don't ask for too much it is much easier. If you want the specifics, it's harder. I want the good life, someone who is not afraid of spending money. I want this because I didn't have too much when growing up.' Then she adds: 'Educated people are easier to be around. They are more upstanding.'

Mei places a premium on education for herself as much as for her men. At least, this was the case until the age of 16 when her clean academic record was sullied a bit.

'In high school I really liked this boy. He was not a top student. When there were class tests I would always leave a few answers blank so that I would not show him up and we could become closer,' she explains, showing how the Chinese attitude that the woman should be below the man in a relationship is all pervasive, even in high school.

It was puppy love between them. Back then people were more conservative, she says, her words an interesting choice, revealing just how fast the pace of change in China is – 'back then' is often used to refer to just five to ten years ago in China, rather than a generation or two before as it might be used in other contexts. As an aside she adds that it has only been in the past year that her parents have gleaned that she is no longer a virgin. Chinese people are still very discreet when it comes to sex. She was appalled when, on a business trip to Xiamen, she was kept up all night by a couple having loud sex next door, and I can tell from this admission and a few others that she is not comfortable talking about sex – like so many Chinese people I have met throughout the years.

Certainly no such action went on with Mei and her high-school boyfriend. They would hold hands, but only in private. It was towards the end of their two-year relationship that they finally kissed.

'He was the dream boy. Tall, skinny (maybe a bit too skinny), good-looking and fun,' she says, her eyes betraying a sense of nostalgia. 'When I look at my journals back then, every day was about him!'

When it came to college, Mei had secured top grades, despite her best attempts to make her boyfriend feel better, and had her pick of places. He, however, continued to struggle and decided to retake the *gaokao*, the college entrance exam. Mei – who could have gone to a top university – instead opted for the next league down, hoping he would follow her a year later. She ended up studying landscape architecture in Beijing, finding herself thousands of miles away from her first love.

She spent the first year of university pining after him. They would regularly write love letters to each other. Then, at the end of the year, she went back home for the summer to see him. It had been 12 months, which might seem like a long time, but in a country the size of China, finding yourself miles away from your loved one for some time is not at all out of the ordinary. One lovingly devoted guy in my office hadn't seen his girlfriend for two years since she had moved to Australia, and had no immediate plans to see her either. The youth of China might be getting richer, yet finding the time and funds to travel is still seen as a luxury and beyond the scope of many.

Mei's reunion with her high-school sweetheart did not go as planned. They went out for lunch and he brought a new girl with him, whom Mei suspects he had been cheating on her with. It was not a second wife; it was a second girlfriend. She broke off their relationship immediately after the lunch.

It was not long before her next compromising situation. Back at university in her second year she met a man in his fifties. He had been divorced for 20 years.

'I fell madly in love with him. He was an architect and a proper gentleman,' she says.

They dated for around five years and he proposed during that time. Unfortunately, the proposal never came to much because he too had a wandering eye.

'One day my phone was dead and I asked to use his phone. I saw all of these numbers calling a girl. He went weird when I asked him about it.'

They rowed for ages, him denying he was cheating, until he eventually confessed. The girl turned out to be his secretary – a cliché, we both remark. Mei was 25 at the time. She was still in love and wanted to get married. It was not meant to be.

The break-up was devastating. The only positive was that she lost lots of weight, she tells me. Mei, who borders on thin, has made several comments throughout our lunch about her calorie intake for the day. It's a fairly typical neurosis amongst Chinese women. Despite the nation's females being much more slender than women from most other nations, young girls in particular still worry about weight. To be fair, diabetes and heart disease are on the rise, as is impotency related to poor diet, according to several recent surveys, and waistlines are bigger now than 20 to 30 years ago as a result of more affluent lifestyles. The previous number-one mode of transport – the bicycle – has been usurped by other, less energetic modes, and diets have changed significantly. Fast-food chains and US junk-food outlets are increasingly becoming a feature of everyday life. Dairy and Western forms of dessert have also entered Chinese diets, all having effects on the nation's waistline. Still, the preoccupation with remaining slim suggests that as China becomes richer, people are starting to challenge the view that weight equals wealth.

Since these two heartbreaks Mei has dated a variety of men, some of them very rich. I asked her if she would rather smile on the back of a bicycle or cry in the back of a BMW, as the famed expression goes.

'Well, with one rich guy we would go to the most expensive restaurants. I had no worries with him. There was no passion, though.' She pauses. 'Smiling in a BMW is better than smiling on a bicycle. However, money wouldn't be the first priority.' At least she is honest about it.

She had her final run-in with infidelity when she changed her settings on her mobile phone app WeChat so that she could see who was around her. People would message and ask her straight out if she wanted to have sex. A lot of people used the app for casual sex. A male friend of hers once had camera sex with a girl from it. Crucially, a lot of men who approached her had wives. The app has since gained a reputation for being the cheating app and Mei can certainly vouch for that. Why does she think that is?

'In China divorce is still a big deal, at least amongst the older generation. Cheating is easier than divorcing,' she offers by way of explanation, adding that the app itself does not create a market for cheating. It is merely another outlet enabling it.

Mei's story might have a happy ending. For the past nine months she has been dating someone whom she hopes is faithful just to her. As she describes her new man a smile creeps over her face. We end the lunch on that positive note. And yet, as she breezes back out through the door, I am left with an impression of a woman who is walking a thin line. On the one hand, she is genuinely trying to be an independent woman, not dictated to by men or familial concerns. She works hard and seems in control, and is clearly a source of pride to her family. On the other hand, she is acutely aware of her limitations and caves in to them sometimes too much. These limitations are a vulnerability shared by many Chinese girls, one which unless tackled quickly will ensure the culture of infidelity continues.

THE GOVERNMENT'S ADULTEROUS RESPONSE

In the face of rising infidelity the government is trying yet another tactic to control it: creating a database of all the married couples in China. The database will first go online in Beijing and Shanghai and will be rolled out nationwide from 2015. It seems like the antithesis of romance, but perhaps doing one's due diligence will save a lot of young people the trouble of falling in love and then having their hearts broken. Certainly a little due diligence would have been handy for Wei Na, the leftover woman from Chapter 1. I catch up with her again a year after she ended her relationship with Yeping. It is a wet, miserable day, which always means one thing: horrendous traffic. Beijing's congestion is notoriously bad. Some of the longest recorded traffic jams in the world have taken place in and around Beijing. On a rainy day, it can reach epic proportions. I opt for the subway, and even this is crowded. At least it is efficient. Minutes later I am in the business district of Beijing and then in a very bright, sterile mall. Finally I arrive at a chain restaurant called Green Tea.

Green Tea is a favourite amongst many Chinese girls I know, since its extensive menu contains many dishes that purport to be both healthy and delicious. It's also a very pleasant spot to hang around in and, much like the French, the Chinese enjoy their long lunch breaks. Those at my work, which was by no means a relaxed environment, would usually take an hour-long lunch break and sometimes even be out of the office for two or three hours.

Wei Na walks through the door with hair twice the length it was the last time we met and an outfit that is just as slinky. One of her work colleagues is beside her, also dressed to the nines and of a similar age. I ask Wei Na whether she is dating anyone at the moment. There is no one on the cards at present, she answers as we tuck into a bowl of steaming silken tofu. Does she ever speak to Yeping, I want to know, and how does she feel about it many months later and now being 30?

'I regretted so much that we were together and that we went on that trip [to Hong Kong]. We were unhappy the whole time. He's so weird with my friends, as you know,' she says.

The friend then injects, 'We are from the same hometown, me and him. But he's so cold. I have never met someone so cold from my hometown.' She gesticulates, adding that in a country as big as China, if you are from the same hometown it means something – there's an instant connection – and yet with Yeping there was nothing.

Wei Na had been in touch with Yeping since they broke up. A few months after, he called her out of the blue. He said he had a good explanation for why he had acted strangely around her friends, and in general.

'He told me he was married! He had been cheating on his wife with me ...' she says, adding: 'Even if he got a divorce, I couldn't think of a future with us. Later on I asked if he had any children. He said yes, he has an eight-year-old son!'

So it turns out Yeping was not a bare branch. Rather, he was a branch with too many leaves. 'What? A wife? A child! How did he conceal this?' I ask, somewhat shocked.

Yeping had used media messages about being a bare branch to his advantage – it was a good cover and distraction. Wei Na would also always go to his work studio, where there was a small bedroom upstairs. She knew he didn't live there. She only chose his studio as it was better located for her. Besides, she never suspected he had a wife and child at home. The thought simply never crossed her mind.

The friend was rolling her eyes at this point, castigating Wei Na for her naivety. 'You can look him up online. I managed to find pictures of him with his son. I always look every guy up I date. Wei Na, you are so easily fooled,' she says, slapping her friend's arm.

'He was also a kind of control-freak, like all Chinese guys. I never suspected,' Wei Na retorts in defence.

The friend continues her attack. Wei Na is perfect *ernai* material, she thinks. 'She doesn't put pressure on them or push and she doesn't go shopping!' she tells me, speaking as if Wei Na isn't sitting right there. She adds that she knows of a 36-year-old second wife who lives in a villa all bought for her by a man. She demands stuff all the time, and this is a normal expectation if you are the bit on the side. Wei Na's lack of demands make her perfect, especially for someone like Yeping who doesn't have a lot of money himself.

The friend bandies around the term *ernai* like it is completely commonplace, so I want to know more. Just how prolific is it amongst her friends?

'It's common. I was at Peking University doing a psychology training course and one of my professors did a survey that found that most middle-aged men went to KTV girls and had better sex. They were not experimental with their wives, whom they had often married more for convenience than love and so sought out sex elsewhere.'

A survey published by the China Sexology Association at the end of 2014 highlighted the level of frustration felt in the bedroom. Over 10,000 male and female professionals across 22 cities in China were asked whether they felt sexually satisfied, with a minority (37 per cent) saying they were 'extremely satisfied' and a majority (51 per cent) saying they were 'basically satisfied'. Many women – 21 per cent – had never experienced an orgasm, while most men said they had sex less than once a week. High pressure in the workforce was cited for the low sexual satisfaction rates, which sounds about right as one of many reasons. The survey did not go into detail about where people were seeking sex when they did have it, but it certainly confirms allegations that a sizable chunk of China's population are not sexually satisfied and the repercussions of this are far-reaching.

Another survey is even more telling. Circulating in the autumn of 2014, it reveals that many men in China find it hard to get hard. The study, entitled 'China Ideal Sex Blue Book', said that Chinese men were suffering high levels of impotence. Just over half of the thousands interviewed were actually achieving full erections, which it described as being 'like a cucumber' (the opposite was referred to as 'like tofu'). Like the other study on good sex, the findings have been challenged, for example by Everett Yuehong Zhang, whose book *The Impotence Epidemic: Men's Medicine and Sexual Desire in Contemporary China* explores this very same topic. He believes that rather than it being an increasing problem, attributed to overstressed modern lifestyles, as the survey concludes, it is merely a sign of Chinese men being more willing to talk about the issue and to seek treatment. Nothing new, in effect. What is new is the willingness to talk about it. To that extent the study reflects the changing nature of desire in China – couples, and indeed individuals, are gradually becoming less tolerant of bad sex.

The fact that plenty of people are still marrying in China out of convenience rather than love (or even, in the least, lust) doesn't bode well for the future of fidelity, especially given the increasing attention paid to good versus bad sex. The government should use its resources in a better way to combat adultery. For example, instead of creating a database it should reduce its messages about leftover women. Allowing people to make better, less rushed and more informed choices could halve the impulse of people to cheat. This, however, would not serve the government's own objectives, not least officials' proclivity to keep mistresses.

So, a year on and still no boyfriend. How are Wei Na's parents and aunt now? Just as nagging as before, apparently, but from a greater distance; Wei Na moved out of her aunt's place at the beginning of the year.

My aunt is happy that I moved out. She thinks if I feel pressure in terms of money, paying rent, I will get married soon. I was too comfortable at home, my aunt and uncle thought. A lot of people think like that – that if you are taken care of too much by family you won't look for and need a husband. My aunt's neighbours told me that too. They knew my age and status even before meeting me the first time and were always saying that I shouldn't live at their home.

For Wei Na it's a different story. She loves living away from her family. She has independence, a great job and great friends. She might be single, but at least that means she isn't dating someone else's husband or being cheated on. The situation is positive for her physical well-being as much as her emotional. Wei Na, and Mei too, are aware of the pitfalls of being a mistress. It's one part glamour and another part risk. Instances of mistresses being beaten up in public circulate, weighing against the comforts that a wealthy man might be able to provide. Then there's the shame attached to an affair that becomes common knowledge. If China allows a mistress culture to thrive, it does not mean the population condone it. Anything that shakes the family-based foundations of Chinese society is frowned upon. Then there's the issue of sex outside marriage. It's still a big deal and something which even the young generation find very difficult to talk about in an honest, open way.

SEX AND
SEXUALITY

6

Let's Talk about Sex

It seems like my government wants people to think of China as the traditional China with Confucian morality and blah, blah, blah. We have these interminable meetings, talk a lot about morality, but when it's all over, people go home and return to their real lives.
Muzi Mei, a prominent Chinese blogger

In 2007, during my first time living in China, my father and sister visited me. We set aside a few days to explore Shanghai before going to see other parts of the country. It was more than enough time. With the main sites done, I booked a trip to visit one of Shanghai's neighbouring water towns. These villages, with their charming courtyard houses and their maze of canals and bridges, are always tonics after spending a while in Shanghai's big smoke. Tongli, the town I selected for my family visit, is no different. Or so I thought.

Alongside Tongli's reputation as being a Venice of the East is another one altogether: Tongli houses China's biggest sex museum.

You wouldn't guess it from walking through the town. Signs for the museum are very discreet. Even in the guidebooks it is a mere footnote on an already slim add-on to a Shanghai trip. And yet, there in Tongli, located inside the walls of a Qing Dynasty garden house, the Museum of Ancient Chinese Sex Culture is located, displaying the history of China's eroticism in all its explicit tumescence. Upon entering through unassuming gates, visitors are greeted by statues of naked men, their huge phalluses jutting into the pathway. The phalluses point in the direction of a series of interconnected rooms in which China's sexual past is stripped bare through narrative and artefact.

At the time I struggled to decipher why China contained such an openly sexual museum and yet placed it in a small town rather than a major metropolis (apparently it was originally in Shanghai and was later moved). Now, some years on from my visit, its location seems symbolic: try as they might to push sex out of sight, it is never completely out of mind in China.

Inherent complications and contradictions in attitudes towards sex have defined China's past as much as they define its present. Although, it should be noted that until the Ming Dynasty (1368–1644) sex in China was more openly embraced, a fact explored in some detail at the museum in Tongli, where 1,000-year-old dildos indicate a playful past.

In recent centuries the trend has been more towards silencing talk – and exploration – of the subject. Governments from the Ming onwards feared chaos. Controlling the population's libido was a good way to control chaos and promote harmony in the country, they believed. Sexual embellishments came to be seen as shameful and inappropriate dinner-table conversation.

And yet even during the Cultural Revolution (1966–76) – one of the peaks of this prudishness when vigour was to be directed towards revolutionary pursuits over those taking place in the bedroom – sex was still very much happening. Hundreds of diary entries and memoirs attest to a raunchy world behind closed doors. Those belonging to the 'sent-down' youth, in particular, spoke of a time of relative sexual freedom as young people lived far away from the watchful eyes of their parents. Needless to say, accounts of teenage pregnancies rose during this period too.

Once the Maoist era came to a close, the country became wealthier, and with that people started to have more time and freedom to explore their sexual identities, and they could do so more openly too. They gained greater agency over their sex lives and premarital sex became a lot more prolific. The 'opening-up' of their sex lives has continued into the twenty-first century, particularly for city dwellers. According to a survey from 2012, over 70 per cent of Chinese have engaged in premarital sex. Some are becoming sexually active as early as middle school, though most experience their first proper sexual dalliance at college as they enter their twenties.

Promiscuity is on the rise. Casual bed-hopping has emerged amongst young urban Chinese in particular, even if the pursuit is still confined to a minority. Seeking guidance from the likes of *Sex and the City*, which started to be peddled at markets from 2003, young Chinese in pursuit of no-strings sex meet partners in bars, nightclubs, karaoke salons and, of late, online and through phone apps.

'The singles are not talking about marriages, and lovers aren't talking about the future,' goes one popular saying among China's youngsters. Another joke describes the pattern of 'one-week' relationships: 'On Monday, you send out vibes. Tuesday, you express true desire. Wednesday, you hold hands. Thursday, you sleep together. Friday, a feeling of distance sets in. Saturday, you want out. On Sunday, you start searching again.'

On top of the increasing frequency of premarital sex, alternatives to marriage are growing in popularity and acceptance. The bulk of young Chinese support the idea of 'trial marriage' or cohabitation, marking a major departure from their parents, who would never have dreamt of such behaviour.

Despite this, having more sex has not translated into a willingness to talk more openly about it. China's conflicted relationship towards coitus stubbornly remains. A female journalist using the pen name of Muzi Mei realised this when she launched her blog 'Leftover Love Letters'. Muzi Mei's warts-and-all account of her sex life was so popular that it knocked Mao Zedong off the list for most searched internet term when it was launched in June 2003. Muzi Mei was 25 at the time and had lost her virginity aged 21. The blog went unnoticed for several months until she posted a lurid account of a dalliance she had with a rock star. After that everyone wanted to read about what she got up to between the sheets. Media from both inside and outside China took note and she pandered to her audience, sparing no details as she told reporters her sexual encounters already numbered in the eighties.

As her celebrity exploded, so too did her critics. *China Youth Daily*, a government-run newspaper, reported that only 10 per cent approved of her lifestyle, against 90 per cent who disapproved. It was not long before her blog was removed from the web and her follow-up book banned within China only days after publication. In the aftermath, Muzi Mei gave an interview to the *Washington Post* in which she said:

> It seems like my government wants people to think of China as the traditional China with Confucian morality and blah, blah, blah. We have these interminable meetings, talk a lot about morality, but when it's all over, people go home and return to their real lives. Most of the propaganda guys I know all have mistresses. Heh, I've even slept with some of them. That's why they're scared of my morality. I know their secrets.

Since Muzi Mei's blog was removed, scores of imitators have taken its place. Another popular blogger, who went by the moniker of Lady Cat, spoke of her sexual journey through an early marriage, speedy divorce and subsequent casual flings. Essays like 'An orgasm a day' outlined her discovery of masturbation and pornography. Similar to her predecessor, it was not long before Lady Cat's blog was removed.

What angers China's censors with all of these blogs is not so much the promiscuity outlined as the openness. Dirty talk outside the bedroom was and still is frowned upon. The message from the government can be summed up as follows: if you are going to sleep around, please don't talk about it.

Why does the government feel so uneasy about conversations on sex? In part it is reflecting public sentiment. Some of the furore caused by these blogs concerned the authors being female. They became embroiled in traditional gender bias in which female sexuality is not celebrated. Men, on the other hand, have more free rein to express and indulge their sexuality, as well as to talk more openly about it.

The recent reaction to *The Vagina Monologues* in Beijing highlights this. Students at a major campus created an online storm in November 2013 when they proceeded to post pictures of themselves holding up messages from their vaginas to the popular social network RenRen, in an effort to promote the play that discusses the very same topic. The messages ranged from 'My vagina says: I want respect' to 'My vagina says: You need to be *invited* to get in.'

A wave of misogyny followed, as the girls' images were re-posted across social and traditional media. Some commentators focused on the women's looks, making derogatory remarks about them. Others were shocked that students could write such things. Others still resorted to slut-shaming.

An 'image that female university students must be pure' was causing the outrage, said Xiao Hang, one of the organisers of *The Vagina Monologues* in an interview with *The Atlantic*. 'They were terrified because women in China never talk about sex in public.'

The Monologues first showed in China ten years ago and each year it is surrounded by some controversy. A professional production in Shanghai was banned in 2004, and a 2009 production was forced to call the show *The V Monologues* instead of its full name. The group in charge of the 2013 show in Beijing discovered that once the word 'vagina' was mentioned official theatres and even some small independent outfits were wary of the show. The play went ahead in the end, though the organisers were aware that they performed to a niche liberal crowd, not a typical, representative one, which would be more akin to those they were confronted with online.

The controversy surrounding *The Vagina Monologues* shows just how uncomfortable Chinese people are when it comes to both the word vagina and female sexuality in general. The celebration of female sexuality is far from complete in the West, but China definitely approaches it in a much more puritanical way; a quick glance through the Chinese edition of *Cosmopolitan* magazine alone reveals these differences when compared to content in its Western counterpart. Those articles that have come to define *Cosmopolitan* in the US and the UK, such as 'How to Obtain the Perfect Orgasm', are simply not in the Chinese magazine.

Women are largely silenced when it comes to conversations about sex, and the sexual gains within the country are mostly for men. But a prudish reluctance to discuss sex has affected everyone overall, whether they have double X chromosomes or not. The increasingly large amount of flesh on display in public is simply misleading.

The government opposition to frank talk probably has other causes. After all, it dovetails nicely with its leftover women campaign and its desire for a harmonious society in which people are married. And the government can hardly justify a ban on pornography if it allows sex talk. It has been unofficially categorised as moral pollution.

Significantly, it is the government's ability to still control conversations about sex which distinguishes China from many other countries. As Richard Burger writes in *Behind the Red Door: Sex in China*:

> While there have been rapid advances in sexual freedom, they are still largely on the government's terms, and that is key to understanding the difference between China's sexual revolution and the one that engulfed the West nearly half a century ago. The Chinese government has made a Faustian bargain with its people to give them freedom in their bedrooms and personal lives in exchange for a government with near-total political control.

As Burger highlights, this pact involves the continued illegality of porn, even if plenty still peddle it, and the censoring of sex from media, not to mention several 'kill the chickens to scare the monkeys' campaigns, as they were commonly referred to in China. For example, in 2010 a computer scientist in Nanjing was jailed for three and a half years on group sex charges for organising a swingers' party – a warning to all who are that way inclined.

Even lighter topics of a sexual note are off-bounds, as Muzi Mei and the girls behind *The Vagina Monologues* have had to learn the hard way (though Muzi Mei later uploaded a 25-minute soundtrack of herself making love, which crashed servers before it was removed). Muzi Mei went on to a job at the newspaper *Southern Metropolis Weekly*, writing about sex and love, just in much tamer form. In the end she signed up to the Faustian bargain too, and her example shows how Chinese people will self-censor if it makes for an easier existence.

SEXUAL HEALTH: TRYING TO TACKLE A PROBLEM YOU CANNOT TALK ABOUT

'I had nothing, absolutely nothing!' says Zhang Lijia, an author and prominent advocate of improved sexual education in China, when I ask her about her own experience of sexual education growing up. 'When I was ten, my neighbour had a baby. I asked my mother where did the baby come from and she said under the arms. I thought, That's strange, because there's no hole there!' she adds.

Zhang came of age in the 1970s when China was undergoing the Cultural Revolution. The following decade, in 1981, the first sex education courses were instated in Shanghai and the Ministry of Education announced they would be established in all middle schools throughout the country.

The sexual education policy coincided with the launch of the One Child Policy. Using contraception became essential. Condoms filled aisles of local supermarkets, where they remain many decades later, often located at the cashiers next to chewing gum as if contraception is an impulse buy.

Still, government messages preach abstention over indulgence – another reason why Chinese people might have more of a puritanical approach to sex. The 1988 sex education charter warned adolescents of the dangers of premarital sex, a message reinforced to this day.

The result is a hotchpotch of sex education policy. Some schools in big urban metropolises offer courses that rival Western counterparts, while others provide no form of guidance – and the trend nationwide is definitely towards the latter rather than the former.

'We've never had a class on sex ed at my school. We're not even allowed to have a boyfriend or a girlfriend. No kissing, nothing,' I was told by an 18-year-old student at a good school in Chengdu, one of China's wealthier and more developed cities. Other people interviewed have been taught little more than the basics. Namely, they learn about anatomical differences between the sexes. They are told that they shouldn't have sex, and that if they do, they must protect themselves. No guidance is given on the nature of protection or why it's necessary.

I speak to Dr Taolin, president of the World Association of Chinese Sexologists, who campaigns for the improvement of sexual education in China. For Taolin, the combination of misinformation and lack of teachers who are qualified on the subject is dangerous. He says that only one university in the country teaches it (Capital Normal University): 'Contradictions arise, for example, contradictions between radical and conservative, right and wrong. The radical may explain the use of condoms in middle school while the conservative still insist on abstinence in college. Someone says puppy love is beneficial, while someone says puppy love should be prohibited.'

Lessons are not taught at home either.

'Parents of children today are still emerging from the cocoon of chastity that Mao wrapped around the Chinese people, and they rarely teach their children about sex education because it would cause embarrassment,' says Richard Burger when I questioned him on the topic. As Burger notes, parents are embarrassed. And they're very focused on their children's grades, as are schoolteachers. Anything distracting from the pursuit of academia is not encouraged.

With few avenues providing tips on sexual basics, Chinese youth are turning to the internet and the arts for help, as the tale of a Beijing student cited in *Slate* in 2009 attested. The article, entitled 'Everything you Always Wanted to Know about Sex (But Didn't Learn Because you Grew Up in China)', opens with an anecdote of a student in the capital:

> The first time Hu Jing tried to have sex with her college boyfriend, there was a technical difficulty. 'We knew we had to use a condom,' she said. 'But we didn't know how.'
>
> Faced with this conundrum, Hu and her boyfriend went looking for answers – he from his more experienced friends, she from the university library, where she combed through *Dream of the Red Chamber*, a literary classic from the Qing Dynasty.
>
> The following week, they reconvened for a second try. This time, they managed to roll on the condom but then … well, where was the penis supposed to go? It took another week of research before they succeeded in doing the deed.

In this case at least they used condoms. Plenty of others do not and a staggering 13 million abortions are carried out on average in China annually. These stats might be an understatement too; many more are believed to be carried out in unregistered clinics. A woman working at a Shanghai pregnancy call centre reported the case of one teenage girl who had undergone 13 abortions to date. Nor do the above statistics speak of those who use some form of morning-after pill.

The failure of attitudes to keep up with actions is having a particularly negative effect in the realms of sexual health. Sexually transmitted infections (STIs) are on the rise. China has particularly high rates of syphilis, while sexual transmission now accounts for 81.7 per cent of all new HIV infections. Much has been made of the widening gap between affluent urban Chinese and the poorer people in the countryside in terms of their accumulation of knowledge overall, including on sex. A knowledge gap certainly exists, but urbanites are still far from wise when it comes to protection – and increasingly risk prone.

It is within this context that I meet Meizhen, a twenty-something girl who conducts research into sexual health as part of her day job. Meizhen is pretty and wears a tight-fitting dress and heels. She is also incredibly open about sex, making her one of a very small handful of Chinese girls I have met who use the word 'fuck' of their own accord. When she does so I am more shocked by its use than she is, so rare is it for me to hear a Chinese girl speak the word. Perhaps her brashness is because we are in a booth when we meet, out of earshot of other punters. Before discussing her sexual health, we start off with small talk. I ask her if she is dating anyone.

'Yes, an actor. The sex is really good.'

My eyes bulge and I can see Meizhen is someone who likes to get a response.

'We started off as friends with benefits. We met five years ago. I'm 28 and he's 40. He was initially cold and we were not in touch. Then we found each other on WeChat this year [the Chinese equivalent of WhatsApp]. Now he is kinda clingy and totally acting like a typical Chinese guy. He's a control freak. He texts every hour and if I don't reply he will accuse me of cheating. This is totally normal for a Chinese guy.' She pauses. 'If I can find another one who will fuck this good, then I will switch.'

Her last statement hangs in the air like a suspended arrow. That Chinese men (and women, for that matter) are controlling, or at least demanding, is something many foreigners struggle with when dating in Beijing. Most people who date locals will have at least one experience of being called constantly from very early on, an immediate level of intensity which they are not used to back home.

'I want to get married, but not with him. He's a kid,' Meizhen continues. 'He has no idea of life goals and always plays computer games on his phone. He requires looking after, a total little emperor. I actually do like to clean, but I don't want him to think I will do this.'

Meizhen goes on to tell me that she has had eight sexual partners in her life, most of whom she never used condoms with. Fortunately, she recently had a sexual health test and is disease-free; moving forward, she is going to take efforts to be more careful.

Meizhen's knowledge of sexual health can be mostly attributed to her job.

'Prior to your job, how much did you know?' I enquire.

Not much at all. The extent of Meizhen's sex education can be summarised in two sentences: 'Our teacher took us to a room and showed a video to us. It was 45 minutes long and explained body differences.'

At least it was something. Plenty of her friends skipped the class about reproduction altogether. Teachers apparently find it very embarrassing to teach and there is no real incentive to do so as it's not an essential part of the syllabus.

However, Meizhen explains that rather than informing herself and her classmates about key aspects of sex, the lesson she did have simply entrenched gender stereotypes – girls as passive, boys as active – and glossed over the rest.

'That is why we have so many abortions. Girls don't know [about sex]. And there are adverts everywhere saying that it [an abortion] is fast and painless.'

Billboards containing adverts from companies that claim to provide 'painless abortions' could once be seen in abundance, sending a message that an abortion is an easy way out with few consequences. The government has recently prohibited these advertisements and yet they still sometimes appear (I would daily cycle past one en route to work) and some small hospitals and clinics offer discounts on the procedure to students if they can provide valid student ID.

As for STIs, this topic is rarely dwelt on in schools, and the result is a nation that is facing a growing problem. On top of looking at sexual health in general, Meizhen has conducted work specifically with the human papilloma virus (HPV) vaccine (only available in Hong Kong at the time of writing). She feels as if she is speaking a different language to her friends when she mentions HPV. It has been an education for her too; working on the vaccine is the only reason she knows about smear tests. Her friends remain in the dark, despite all being in their late twenties and sexually active. If anecdotes from my foreign friends of their trips to a Chinese gynaecologist are anything to go by, plenty of Chinese doctors are in the dark too about what is going on down there. I've heard horror stories of doctors hardly knowing how to conduct a standard smear test, which no doubt put those who do know about smear tests off getting checked regularly.

'No one ever told us, not even the teacher. If I wasn't on that project, I wouldn't have known,' she continues on smear testing.

Meizhen is lucky that she is able to learn about the fundamentals of sexual health from her job. Otherwise she would be clueless, like so many other young Chinese. Prior to this job, the basics that Meizhen was able to garner came from the entertainment industry and general trial and error. For the most part it was Western entertainment, not Chinese; the latter is so tightly restricted that kissing is often as racy as it gets. No surprise then that there are stories of college-age kids in China asking if kissing leads to pregnancy. A glossy veneer on sex, as is often placed on it in most Hollywood films, does nothing to teach Meizhen and her contemporaries about the real ins and outs.

The inability to talk about sex in an honest, open manner has other consequences. Females, in particular, are in a vulnerable position. A total of 125 cases of sexual assaults on children were reported in 2013, while in a report from the same year conducted by the UN a staggering 22.2 per cent of 998 Chinese male respondents said that they had raped a woman, including a partner.

'With so little sex education and knowledge, you become very vulnerable to abuse,' Zhang, the author, tells me; she is herself a victim of child sexual abuse.

Misinformation spurs other, bizarre, results. One of the greatest examples of China's ability to mix Western with

Eastern and old with new is the continued prevalence of traditional Chinese medicine (TCM). TCM is institutionalised in China, to the extent that in 2012, TCM companies received an extra $1 billion (over £650 million) in government money. In pharmacies, TCM medicines share shelf space with more conventional treatments. Staff rarely differentiate between the two. I've learnt the hard way: upon catching the flu several years back, I went to a Chinese pharmacy to procure standard over-the-counter medicine. Knowing that antibiotics are readily available in China, I stressed my allergy to penicillin. Ten confusing minutes later I left with a variety of plants in pill form.

The youth of China hold on to the values of TCM. Even educated people rarely challenge these centuries-old traditions and some have their entire lifestyle dictated by them. People in my office were constantly prescribing different treatments and medicines in accordance with TCM. Seasonal shifts meant changes in diet; more serious ailments were treated with cocktails of boiled herbs.

TCM permeates Chinese popular thinking about health, and this includes sexual health. Meizhen's mother, for example, suggested she take a certain type of traditional Chinese medication because she believed it would help her circulation, and in turn, fertility. She was fretting that her 28-year-old daughter was running out of time. Meizhen had not heard of the medication and went to a doctor to ask for advice. She was quickly informed that it was only prescribed for the menopause and could be dangerous for her. She stopped taking it immediately.

Meanwhile, the belief in *qi*, energy, which is fundamental to the values of TCM, has provoked a shortage of sperm donations in China. Sperm is associated with *qi* (Chinese traditional culture says one drop of semen is as precious as ten drops of blood) and so giving it away is perceived as dangerous. Excessive ejaculation means loss of much more blood, which is harmful to health. And plenty of young men continue to eat the penis of animals in the hope their virility will be improved. In the absence of adequate education on sexual reproduction, these theories can run wild.

That said, early on in 2014, the government issued a teaching outline for sex education lessons, providing step-by-step guidance for teachers on how to teach primary-school children. At the same time as the guide was released, two members of the Chinese People's Political Consultative Conference (CPPCC) National Committee suggested making sex education part of the compulsory education curriculum.

Is there going to be a change in attitude amongst those Chinese children coming of age now? Will the teachers offer proper, informative classes on sex education or will they be too embarrassed and shirk their responsibilities once again? One hopes that they will go through with it. As the high-school girl interviewed at the start of this chapter attests, a whole generation of children are about to come of age who remain none the wiser. It's appalling when you consider that Chinese youth represent one-fifth of the world's youth. When it comes to sex, at least 20 per cent of us remain in the dark. And yet, as China is learning, once Pandora's Box is opened, it's hard to close. The government needs to act soon, or face the consequences of being out of sync with what's going on in Chinese bedrooms.

7

Sex, Drugs, Rock and Roll

When you walk on the street everyone looks like a virgin, but they all have sex. I did a survey of porno sites and discovered many career people doing kinky, perverted things.
Viktor, sex-toy entrepreneur and lead singer in Bedstars

Chinese youth are experimenting outside the bedroom as much as they are inside. As an increasingly hedonistic bunch, their slogan could well be *Carpe Diem* or, more accurately, *Carpe Noctem*. At night, the country's cities hum to the noise of fancy bars and clubs, underground raves and private parties. People cite New York as the city that never sleeps, but in the twenty-first century, such a label should really be awarded to Shanghai first, and Beijing second.

The strict moral codes which were created by Confucius and adapted by the Communists are dissolving around China. Since the 1980s, waves of 'spiritual pollution' from outside China have washed over the nation's youth, who have proved more than ready to embrace these influences. Replacing Communist jargon and imagery, China's now-open doors have allowed in new role models, such as pop stars from Hong Kong, Taiwan and the US. Young people have stepped out of their Maoist straightjackets and started to enjoy more daring choices in their clothing and lifestyles.

Viktor and his friends are certainly in thrall to Beijing's new hedonism. They symbolise the possibilities open to Chinese youth who choose to experiment. Viktor is the lead singer in a Beijing-based band called Bedstars – the name is not a coincidence – and is very immersed in China's underground rock scene. Describing themselves as 'doomsday rock', Bedstars' influences range from The Rolling Stones through The Libertines. On top of music, Viktor is trying to bring about a sexual revolution in China through launching his own sex-toy company.

I meet Viktor on a warm Wednesday afternoon. He sends me to a guitar shop in a hip, central area of town. The shop is the smallest in a row of guitar stores – it is barely the size of an average bathroom – and is located on a street dominated by dive bars and offbeat boutiques. Guitars cover the tiny wall area and a flag of the Sex Pistols' album *God Save the Queen* peeks out from between them.

Perched on a tiny plastic stool is John, a scrawny boy with hair dyed dark orange. I quickly deduce he is the band's drummer. To a soundtrack of jazz, he uses one hand to balance a cigarette and the other to surf through a playlist on his computer. One of his colleagues, Ricky, soon appears.

'Oh you're English! You're English! I have been to England!' he enthuses. It transpires that Ricky and John are former bandmates in a group called Rustic, which won the Global Battle of the Bands in 2009, a big accolade and one that took them to England. The boys are originally from rural northern China and describe themselves as farm boys. Like other ambitious young people, they moved to the capital to try and make it. This background of struggle features in many of their songs, such as one called 'Rock n Roll for Money and Sex'. It is a song about their projected desires, which have arguably come true (just not quite in a Mick Jagger way).

Winning the competition in London was certainly a dream. From their humble beginnings they beat 19 other countries in a showdown; it was their first time overseas, and they took home a gold trophy and a cash prize worth more than they could ever imagine. Li Fan, another band member, was 21 at the time of winning and Ricky was 19. No Chinese band had ever done this before.

Ricky points to another poster, also hidden behind guitars on the wall. It is of Rustic back in their glory days. 'Do you recognise us?' he asks.

I squint, my eyes flicking back and forward between the two. Ricky is tall and has a pretty face, in an androgynous way. He is wearing Converse shoes, a T-shirt, and despite the temperature being 30 degrees, a pink, purple and yellow jacket. His hair, which is reasonably short, has a subtle purple hue running through and one of his ears is pierced. The aesthetic is not flamboyant. In the poster, on the other hand, three heavily made-up Marilyn Manson types glare into the camera lens. Ricky specifically has hair that makes him look like Edward Scissorhands. The picture bears no resemblance to the happy-go-lucky boys standing in front of me.

As I tell them this, the music changes to electro-rock and John gets up to switch places with Ricky. Ricky moves to the computer and puts on a song for me to listen to. It is Rustic.

'We sang in English,' he explains. 'Bad English!'

'It's better to sing in English because it's more cool. And rock is Western too, so it makes sense. It's hard writing song lyrics because I'm not a native English speaker. So I have to translate when writing the lyrics,' he tells me, saying how as a child he would write songs in Chinese, but now he never does.

'No kids in China care about rock. They're more into pop. I of course love it because it's more free. There's no pretending. Society is more about money now. I think that's everywhere, though,' he says, shrugging.

'What do you think of the rock music culture now?' I ask.

Aged 20 to 30 people in China don't have a good music culture. At school they teach you how to play music but not what music is. Music should play from the heart. It should be for yourself, not for an audience. In China people like me can't become really good musicians because there is no music education or innovation. We keep on copying from the West. Maybe one day they [the West] will stop making music and we will catch up. We only started playing in the 1980s, whereas the West started what, the end of the 1940s? So the music scene in China is like the equivalent of the seventies and eighties in the West.

Ricky pauses, then sighs. 'Even though I'm turning 25, I'm still poor about music. I wanna know so much more so I'm listening to more. I wanna have my own style eventually.'

It is true that rock music in China is not as old as in the West. It has, however, taken on some unique tones, as Jonathan Campbell describes in his book *Red Rock: The Long, Strange March of Chinese Rock and Roll*. He writes:

international media reports on China's contemporary urban culture – skateboarding, punk music, experimental theatre – abound, but rarely delve beneath the 'hey-check-this-out-they're-doing-stuff-we-did!' quickie. Yes, there was a journey from Mao to mohawks, but as much as the alliteration may work, there's far more to the story than what's at the surface.

Campbell articulates over the course of his book the strange and wonderful quirks of Chinese rock music, which goes by the name of *yaogun*, a banner used to group many different people and musical styles.

Back in the guitar store with Ricky, his self-deprecation spreads to the topic of his girlfriend. She works in contemporary art and has different tastes to him. Just as he starts to tell me about how they got together, Viktor shows up. At his side is a girl, waif thin, in teeny hot pants that leave little to the imagination. Bulky black platforms, a red T-shirt and a dainty bag are thrown in the mix. It is an interesting combination: part athletic, part punk and part princess. Chinese girls certainly have fun with fashion.

We decide to grab a drink on the rooftop of a café around the corner. After walking through a labyrinth of lanes, we arrive at an industrial-chic restaurant. Despite holding a lit cigarette, Viktor walks straight in, ignores the waiter and marches up a narrow flight of stairs to a makeshift rooftop terrace, choosing a table in the corner.

'I don't think there's such a thing called Chinese rock music,' he tells me, after explaining that his band, Bedstars, is so named because it sounds 'slutty'.

Viktor was born in Henan, in central China, and raised at a military base as his dad was an officer. There were lots of other children at the base, which suited Viktor as he always longed for an older sister to play with. Then, at the age of 15, he moved to Beijing, where he has now been for 11 years.

'I'm a lousy singer and player. For rock music you don't need skills but passion,' says Viktor, whose band is known for its head-banging music and crowd surfing. Viktor's passion comes from noise, lots of it, and beats, he tells me. Most of all his passion comes from girls.

'Are girls into rock stars like they are back home?'

'Nah, the girls here are into pop shit. They don't wanna date a rock star,' he says, adding that girls rarely hit on him. 'It's because I'm ugly,' he remarks. To be honest, Viktor is not the most attractive man I have met. Looks are not working on his side and neither is the music culture of China, which as yet is free from a culture of professional groupies, though some girls are starting to desire people in rock.

'What do you think about groupies?' I turn to ask his girlfriend. She has been sitting with us the whole time playing on her phone and chain-smoking. At this question she rolls her eyes. 'I don't judge. Everyone has their own life. But I would never act like that myself,' she says matter-of-factly, an air of condescension around her words.

Viktor and his girlfriend are currently living at his parents' place. It is a temporary arrangement while the girlfriend, unemployed, applies for jobs. Being a music editor is the dream, she says. Viktor's parents are okay with the living situation. Like other Chinese parents, their gripe is merely that their son is not yet married, and shows no intention of changing this situation. The girlfriend's parents, on the other hand, do not know that she is living with her boyfriend. In fact, they don't even know she has a boyfriend. They live in the southern province of Hunan. China is depressing, she explains, Hunan particularly so. The province is suffocating as a result of the attitude of the people, who are less tolerant towards difference. Her parents want her to follow a conventional route: make money and get married. Beijing is a more tolerant city and allows her to veer off the beaten track, which is exactly why she has ended up here.

China's capital is more liberal – that part is true. It is also accommodating of creativity. But only to a degree. Bands come and go and in Beijing, as in the rest of China, *guanxi* – connections – rule supreme. There is nothing easy about making it in China, even if there are plenty more opportunities. The stories of struggle from Viktor, his girlfriend and his friends highlight this point.

Before moving on to the topic of his sexual revolution, I want to hear a bit more about Viktor's band. What does he sing about, I first ask? Apparently songs about the life he lives. One song in particular is about the sad and upset faces he sees daily on the subway.

'The people, they close their eyes. They don't look happy, even if they might be going back to a home with a wife and kid.'

This is another truth. Rush hour in Beijing is a nightmare, nowhere more so than on the subway, where most of the city's 20 million-plus workers try to cram onto a system that does not have the capacity. Those with a proclivity to commuter rage are best advised to avoid it.

And of course he sings about love, about girls breaking his heart and him breaking theirs. As the conversation steers onto this topic, I look back and forth between Viktor and his girlfriend. She is growing increasingly uncomfortable.

'I used to sing about drinking too, but now I've quit [drinking]. I hurt people when I drink. I hurt my girlfriend. I kissed another girl right in front of her. Didn't even remember!' he says chuckling to himself as the opposite reaction takes hold of his girlfriend's face.

'What do you think about this?' I ask her.

She stubs out a cigarette and looks away.

What Viktor does not write or sing about is politics, which makes sense if you want your band to survive and avoid government harassment. It's part of the Faustian bargain mentioned earlier: the Communist government will grant youth a degree of freedom in their personal lives so long as they don't ask for too much.

'I don't know anything about politics. I don't care about it. I used to love the idea of China having democracy. But then I think there is no solution. The current government looks ugly. They're all fat and they look like bad people.'

Bo Xilai is good-looking, I throw into the chat as a counterpoint.

'There's a joke in China about his name. It sounds like bullshit lie. They're [the government] not stupid, but they give the impression they're stupid. They're smart in a bad way,' Viktor chips in, revealing that perhaps he does care about politics more than he would like to concede. Viktor's is a common enough stance, and one which will be explored in more detail later. The bulk of twenty-somethings in China occupy a middle ground between caring about politics and being completely uninvolved. They can largely see through the indoctrination, they are alert to the key issues, yet they're unwilling to challenge the status quo. In short, they like democracy as a concept, just not quite now. Now is for fun, for not asking for too much.

As we veer away from music, I bring up the topic of sex. Viktor feels somewhat short-changed when it comes to the cliché of sex, drugs, rock and roll. In China the first two are much less dominant and money is a constant problem. If Viktor continues along the rock music trajectory, he calculates, getting enough money to afford the Beijing rents is unlikely in the near future. The industry is still too underground and, without enough financial support, he will always struggle. Those who are able to stay in the game are often kids who are bankrolled by their parents. He knows of people who haven't even produced a single record and yet they have their own line of T-shirts and other paraphernalia as they try to copy what they perceive to be norms of the Western music industry.

It's not all doom and gloom in China's music industry. For every negative anecdote, there is a counter-example of a good band in China, and the entertainment industry is becoming more diversified. Contrary to the stories that circulate in the national media, and to arguments I have heard from other Chinese, Viktor actually thinks the youth of today are becoming less materialistic. Those born in the 1990s onwards are a different species from those born in the 1980s, immediately after the opening-up, he believes. They have different wants, different music tastes and – interestingly – different bedroom habits.

SAFE SEX SELLS

Unwilling to put all his energy into just music, Viktor has found another avenue to channel his interests and ambitions: the sex-toy industry. Viktor is currently in the process of starting an online sex store, which will sell toys and kinky underwear. For him, a revolution is underway and the revolution comes in the form of a dildo.

Online is the perfect platform in China for something sexy, he tells me. Chinese people are still very conservative. Walking into a store is embarrassing; online avoids that. So embarrassed are the Chinese about their sex lives that, according to his calculations, condoms will be the biggest sellers. The condoms at the cashiers are decorative; people rarely want to buy them so publicly.

'When you walk on the street everyone looks like a virgin, but they all have sex. I did a survey of porno sites and discovered many career people doing kinky, perverted things,' he exclaims, leaning across the table and looking me straight in the eyes.

'*Shi hen ku*' – 'It's very cool' his girlfriend chips in, *ku* being a transliteration of its English counterpart.

It is hard to tell if Viktor's idea really is that revolutionary. Beijing is littered with sex stores. Others cottoned on to the market potential a while back. As for the demand side, people must be frequenting these stores to keep them in business. Chinese people can't all be as shy as Viktor assumes. Later on, with this in mind, I venture into one myself. The shop assistant looks at me with utmost suspicion when I start asking a series of questions. He's frugal with information, only revealing that the shop has an even split of foreign and Chinese customers (note: I am the only customer in there at the time). The shop is not too far from some major hotels and also stocks fancy dress, which might explain the even split. My suspicions are that elsewhere in the city, the ratio of Chinese to foreigners would be higher.

A cursory glance elsewhere reveals that the sex-toy market in China is booming. While most people do not partake in one-night stands or have the number of partners that their youthful counterparts have in the West, they are becoming increasingly adventurous and this translates into a sex-toy industry in full swing. China is estimated to make 80 per cent of the world's sex toys, with 1 million people employed in the industry. In the past these products have largely left the country. Now they're staying put.

Adam and Eve was the first ever sex-toy store in China, opening in Beijing in 1993. Two decades later Beijing houses more than 2,000 sex stores. Definitive figures for the size of China's sex-toy market are difficult to come by, but some speculate. For example, a 2012 article in Chinese business magazine *The Founder* places it at $16 billion (£10.5 billion). The domestic market is on the up, with the Chinese version of men's magazine *GQ* calculating the market's annual growth at 63.9 per cent.

This says nothing of online, Viktor's future office. If you go onto Taobao, China's equivalent of eBay, you find thousands of stores willing to cater to the sexually curious or deviant. How does Viktor intend to differentiate himself? Apparently by reversing the trend: importing foreign toys.

'China is the factory of the world and things made here are bad quality. People want good quality. They will pay more,' he says with conviction.

Viktor raises a good point. Quality control is a huge issue in modern China. The most famous example remains the milk scandal of 2008, and that's of the ones that have made it into Western headlines. Chinese newspapers are regularly filled with stories about such scandals. Still more never make it into print. One of the simultaneously high and low points of working at a state-controlled newspaper was that I would hear much of the news going on in China before it got erased from public record. Several times during my year at the paper new scandals circulated only to be quickly crushed as they were deemed 'too sensitive' or someone had been paid off.

If Viktor really is onto something, then the world should be worried. Exploding vibrators do not sound safe. With this image in mind, I speak to Brian Sloan, an American who moved to China several years ago to export sex toys to the West. Does he have issues with quality control, I ask him? Not really, he responds quickly.

'Quality control is handled the same as with any other product. For large orders I would use a secondary inspection company to do their own QC. Normally the factory handles it by itself. The factories who make sex toys do not want to make dangerous products, because then they wouldn't have repeat customers.'

Sloan explains that his clients have different quality-level requirements. They can use extremely safe or relatively less safe materials.

'But I don't think anyone would make something totally unsafe to use. The safeness of materials relate mostly to how easy they are to clean and what chemicals are in them.'

Condoms are a totally different industry he adds, one which Sloan is not involved in. Stories of 'faulty' condoms have made headlines regularly, and these stories are not limited to China's borders. In April 2013 more than 110 million faulty Chinese-made condoms were seized in Ghana. The condoms had holes and burst easily. In another condom-related news story police in China confiscated over 2 million condoms which were being palmed off as Durex, Contex and Jissbon, a popular brand whose name is meant to sound like James Bond. Importing real Durex isn't such a bad idea in light of this.

The perception that Chinese products are faulty is strong, and thus Viktor might have come up with a jackpot idea. In the least he thinks that those that he mocks so much – the rich kids with no idea – will go in for more exclusive sex products. Western products have a lot of cachet in the Chinese market. Plenty of leading designers have moved their main factories to China to export to the rest of the world while maintaining small operations outside China to import into the country because having a label reading 'Made in Italy' or elsewhere is more likely to sell. Time will tell whether the same applies to other, more intimate products which are less for show.

Like most aspects that we touch on during our conversation, Viktor is light-hearted when it comes to China's various scandals, brushing them off with humour. He pokes fun at the fact that he will potentially die younger in Beijing (recent statistics say that those living in north China should expect to live for 5.5 years less than their southern counterparts because of air quality). He jokes that living amidst low-level toxicity, as he calls it, makes him stronger.

'Have you heard about the tour group of Chinese and Japanese people visiting India? The Japanese get ill but the Chinese are fine because they're immune,' he says, laughing.

His girlfriend, meanwhile, is less amused by it all. 'It's depressing…in every way,' she says, stamping out the fifteenth cigarette she has smoked since I met them.

Both their attitudes are interesting. Since the Tiananmen Square Massacre in 1989, the legitimacy of the government amongst China's youth has largely hinged on its ability to provide them with better, richer lives. As prices skyrocket in the country, making everything increasingly unaffordable, and pollution becomes a real, tangible threat, the future is looking less certain for the Party. Even if it maintains control, the existence of people like Viktor and his cohort show that not all swallow the government line and think in just one way. There are limits to approaching Chinese youth as one monolithic group and assuming the deal of freedom in personal lives for silence politically will go unbroken.

The interview winds down and I finally want to know what their future will entail. Will they get married and appease their parents? The girlfriend is a romantic, wanting the till-death-do-us-part bit. Viktor is more a cold realist: 'If you love each other it doesn't matter if you get married. It's just for economy. My mum is so worried. She's always saying, "Why can't you be like other people? All I want is you to be normal!" I tell her my future is unwritten.'

I playfully joke that they are both almost 26 and the clock is ticking, especially for the girl. '*Sheng nu* tick-tock tick-tock!'

'Fuck them who care about *sheng nu*!' Viktor spits, growling at the waiter for the bill.

Done with coffee, we head back to the guitar shop. We walk past a new bar and Viktor pauses, peering through the window. 'I thought you no longer drank because it makes you misbehave?' I enquire.

Yeah, and because I'm on medication. Me, my mother and my girlfriend are all on anti-depressants. We are all depressed! My mother is depressed because she is so disappointed that her son is in a profession that earns no money, that I dropped out of school and that I am not interested in marriage. My girlfriend is depressed because I keep on cheating on her. And I'm depressed because my mum and girlfriend are depressed. My dad, though, he's a happy man.

Moments later we arrive at the guitar store. A girl is outside, clad in school uniform and looking roughly the age of ten. She is screaming at her mum, saying she wants to watch TV. Her mother is screaming back at her saying she needs to do her homework. Viktor laughs, likening the situation to his own childhood, and I am reminded once again that for all the change in China, there is still continuity. With that I unchain my bike, which is parked outside. Viktor starts gossiping away with his bandmate and friends, who are both in the same spot where I had left them earlier. More cigarettes are lit and to a background of screams and laughter I cycle off into the night.

GETTING HIGH:
THE ASCENT OF A DRUG CULTURE

Pharmaceutical drugs and cigarettes aside, one of the topics that Viktor and I do not discuss is recreational drugs. I suspect that, if we had, our conversation would have been lively. Jonathan Campbell documents the rise of recreational drugs in *Red Rock*. Drugs and rock go hand in hand in China as much as they do elsewhere.

With more relaxed borders, increased wealth and greater individual freedoms, drug taking is becoming a permanent fixture within certain pockets of Chinese society. In an anonymous survey I conducted as research for this book, sent out to 50 people ranging from 18 to 30, 16 per cent of the respondents said they either had done drugs or knew someone who had. Most – 96 per cent – said they didn't think taking drugs was cool, though they were evenly divided over whether drug users should be punished or not. Marijuana was singled out as okay, particularly if used for medicinal purposes.

Such mixed reactions were also displayed back in August 2008, when news of the 'Lost Heart' blog hit the press. It was penned by an 18-year-old girl with drug addiction and suicidal tendencies. When you click into the website, electronic music starts to play, the groaning and heavy breathing of a man imitating a woman then takes over and the following caption appears: 'The room has been booked, the foil placed, the ice pipe prepared. The fire is burning, the ice is running, let's start, shall we?'

The site is filled with images of gaunt girls and heavily tattooed men snorting drugs through straws.

The reaction to the blog was mixed. Some expressed sympathy for the blogger and her friends, relating that they too knew drug users; others expressed horror that this was going on and even called for a search to find those who were fuelling her addiction. The girl spoke of Triad members, and people were keen to chase the online paper trail.

Several years later, illegal drugs are moving away from the margins of the blogosphere and closer to the centre of youthful socialising. According to the Brookings Institution, the number of officially registered addicts increased from 70,000 in 1990 to more than 1.79 million at the end of 2011. In reality, the number of actual addicts might run as high as 12 million. It's likely that the government suppresses statistics. Moreover, the distinction between addicts and users in China is not clearly outlined, further complicating the issue.

The increased popularity of drugs is certainly evident in Beijing. Getting drugs in the city is easy. One only needs to head to Sanlitun, a central going-out area, and men peddling drugs will probably approach you. While these men rarely solicit Chinese over expats, sources tell me that scoring drugs is not difficult for locals either. If some of the parties I have been to are anything to go by, I can believe that.

Until recently heroin has been the drug of choice when it comes to Class A drugs, with marijuana being widespread in both 'druggy' circles and 'non-druggy' circles. Then, around 2010, synthetic drugs such as methamphetamine, ecstasy and ketamine, and other hard drugs such as cocaine, started to compete in popularity. The drugs are coming from North Korea, international transport hubs and home-grown labs. Young, wealthy urbanites as well as rural youth are the main users, with people under 35 making up more than 80 per cent of all addicts.

Han Dan, Associate Professor at the Department of Sociology at Jiangsu Administration Institute, who conducted research into drug use and AIDS risks in China, commented in the *Global Times*: 'In my opinion, the subculture created by new drug users stems from the youth's pop culture of hedonism and consumerism [...] to many Chinese youths, Western pop culture means experiencing happiness, physical pleasure and an open attitude toward sex. All these could be realized through taking designer drugs.'

Meth is becoming particularly common, most notably within the gay community. A friend tells me: 'They all ask on Jack'd if you want to have fun and if you have any ice [meth], at which point I usually block them or say goodbye.'

During my first time in a gay club in China, back in 2006 in Shanghai, the room was full of patrons snorting poppers. Experimentation has now migrated to meth. Crystal meth is commonly referred to as *bing*, meaning ice, and 'doing meth' is called *liu bing*, or 'ice skating'. Initially it was confined to the rural hinterland. It took off amongst populations not previously pegged as drug users, such as truck drivers, who smoked it to stay awake for days on long-distance journeys. Now it's starting to penetrate urban areas as a party and sex drug. Its increased popularity is in part due to the ease with which it could be made and obtained in the country. Procuring the key ingredients in the manufacture of meth is comparatively easy in China. *Ephedra sinica*, the shrub that is used in meth production, is native to the country. The plant has been used for centuries in traditional Chinese medicine. Other ingredients and tools are also readily available. Crucially, China is a huge source of precursor chemicals such as ephedrine and pseudoephedrine, which are also used to create methamphetamine.

The explosion of drugs within China has posed a problem for the government, which has adopted various methods of tackling it. Record-breaking drug busts happen frequently and executions of dealers are broadcast around the nation to act as a warning. Sometimes only small amounts of substances were found on people who were given the death penalty. These tactics certainly scared some: I've met young people who are very cautious about how and where they score drugs. Some are put off altogether in ways that they might not be if they were in the UK or other countries with lighter sentences.

The government's harsh line on drugs continues a long tradition. China has bitter memories of the opium wars, which took place in the middle of the nineteenth century, and holds those historical figures who fought against it in high esteem. Lin Zexu, a Qing Dynasty official who initiated a war against British opium when most Chinese authorities tacitly allowed it, remains widely honoured and respected in China. Modern Chinese attitudes towards drugs, at least amongst the older generations, contain strains of Lin's approach. The puritanical view is visible even in the contours of Chinese censorship. On social media, searches for marijuana and specific slang for other drugs such as ketamine are blocked, perhaps owing to the increased use of the internet to facilitate drug deals.

But, like its policy on sex education, more often than not the government embarks on half-measures. For example, regarding meth in particular, ID is required for people buying medicines containing ephedrine and pseudoephedrine, and caps are placed on how much consumers can purchase at any one time. Enforcement is patchy, though, and plenty of pharmacies circumvent the rules.

Several local governments are also coming up with creative ways to combat usage. Sponsoring online dialogues and information campaigns, especially those targeted at youth, is one such way. In the city of Tianjin next to Beijing, for example, various civic organisations have partnered with the city government to host a viral anti-drug campaign on Weibo, asking youth to repost anti-drug messages to three of their friends. Participants are entered in a raffle for the chance to win an iPad, iPods and other electronic goods. The campaigns are not just about curbing drug use; they are about curbing misinformation. Myths that certain drugs are not addictive, that they help with weight loss and improve sexual prowess are all circulating, adding to the appeal of drugs amongst China's youth.

Even though drug-taking is not quite on the same scale as in the US and UK, everything needs to be put in perspective. The twentieth century in China saw an eradication of the country's opium past. Only 25 years ago, narcotics and illicit drug use were practically unheard of. When they were mentioned, it would invite consternation. Herein lies an irony: the escalation of drug use amongst Chinese kids has been provoked by the country's relatively drug-free past. While my parents, for example, might not have been experimenting with acid at Woodstock, they were still kids of the 1960s and 1970s and all that entailed. Not so for the parents in China, who had zero exposure to drugs growing up. The result is once again discord between children and parents, with the latter offering minimal empathy and guidance to the former.

Meanwhile, Chinese youth are starting to experiment with less conventional drugs for other reasons. I've heard of school kids who sniff smelling salts in order to keep themselves awake during their studies. These are extreme examples. Most channel their addictions into caffeine or endless hours of computer games, of the more typical bad habits.

This chapter has shown how Chinese youth are experimenting with sex, drugs and music in ways that would have been inconceivable to their parents' generation. Their behaviours are increasingly daring and individual. It is within this context that previously suppressed sexualities are able to be expressed, which we turn our attentions to now.

8

Half out of the Closet
Being Gay in Twenty-First-Century China

*I was using Chanel lipstick one time at home
and my mum asked me why I was not wearing
Max Factor. I was like, Mum why aren't you
asking me whether I am gay?*
*Zong, who works in business development
at an art gallery*

It is a biting cold evening in December when I find myself queuing to get into Destination, the biggest gay club in Beijing. Destination is located in an area renowned for its clubs. They are all huge, a reflection of the city they are in, and they are very bling. One was once aptly described to me as resembling the inside of a Rolex watch, since it shimmers with gold.

As I wait, all I can think about is the weather. It is the kind of cold that consumes your thoughts and conversation, the kind of cold where even the soles of your feet feel it. As the temperature continues to drop outside, the opposite is happening inside. The night is just warming up. We are soon ushered indoors. A maze of rooms unfolds before me. First a bar area, where pricey cocktails are being served en masse. Up a flight of stairs is another lounge area, which doubles as a venue for edgy art during the day. Back around a corner the clubbing area is housed, a large dance floor which is literally on springs. If you stand still you bounce up and down. A mix of house and disco blasts from the speakers.

On an average Friday or Saturday night, more than 800 people cram into the four-storey nightclub and this night is no exception. The various rooms continue to fill up with men in their twenties or thirties who aren't shy of spending big on a big night out. Edward Yang, one of five co-founders of Destination, said that he and his partners' main motive in opening the nightclub was to provide a platform for gay people to socialise. Yang, who worked full-time as an accountant for a multinational firm, was excited about investing just under 1 million yuan (£100,000) to become a partner in the business and, judging by this night, his investment has paid off.

Destination is one of several gay venues in Beijing and has garnered a reputation for attracting in-the-closet Communist Party officials amongst its clientele. Shanghai has even more establishments. When I lived there in 2007, the city was full of gay bars and clubs, alongside more nuanced venues, such as bear bars and a café-turned-clothing store for gay people. The scene has become more vibrant and dynamic with each passing year. Beijing has failed to keep up numerically. It is superficially less active and the number of bars and clubs for gay people can be counted on the fingers of one hand. However, the scene has other strengths: namely, it is the political locus, the nucleus of discussions on gay rights in the country.

None of this existed 20 years ago. Homosexuality has only been legal in China since 1997. Its history is complex and in many ways surprising. For centuries China was among the most tolerant nations towards homosexuals. Throughout most of its 5,000-year history, China not only tolerated homosexuality, it celebrated it, with references to same-sex liaisons in literature being common.

Some have suggested that the difference in the treatment of homosexuality in China compared to many other parts of the world lies in China's lack of religious affiliation. The famous German sociologist Max Weber controversially thought the country's lack of a Protestant work ethic was holding it back in terms of industrialisation at the start of the twentieth century. For the most part this argument has been discredited. What is less controversial to say is that without a governing book in China such as the Bible, China has been spared certain causes of homophobia. Confucianism is the nearest the Chinese have to a state-wide religion and within Confucianism there are no teachings that say homosexuality is a sin. Rather, Confucianism is about fulfilling filial duty. Providing you get married and have children, you have lived true to the main tenets. What you do in your spare time is your own business.

As a result, homosexuality was not perceived as something deviant or psychologically disturbing in the way it has been historically seen in the West, particularly in the West's religious circles. There was not even a term for homosexuality in the past, and the practice was rarely criticised. Plenty of men had liaisons with other men and, for the nobility, it was even expected at times that they would take young male lovers in addition to their wives.

As this indicates, where the stigma of homosexuality came from was the family. With pressure to marry and have children, homosexuality was accepted so long as it did not interfere with procreation and the 'natural' order of things. When it did it was frowned upon. One of the most popular sayings in traditional Chinese culture is: 'Of the kinds of unfilial behaviour, no offspring is the worst.' Therefore homosexuals still didn't have an easy ride in Imperial China as they were expected to procreate with members of the opposite sex.

Views about homosexuality started to change around the time of the last empire, the Qing (1644–1911). Widely known for their puritanical attitude compared to the fairly liberal Ming Dynasty that immediately preceded them, Qing rulers were very concerned about fixed gender roles and a belief that sex should only be between husband and wife. Laws were instituted to ban sex outside marriage, which included homosexual sex.

The nineteenth century saw an influx of Westerners into China. Christian missionaries came preaching the Bible, including its homophobic messages. Then, in 1860, the British and French defeated the Qing emperor in the Second Opium War, with certain parts of the nation being ceded to them through harsh treaties. It was a defining moment in the country's history, one which is still often brought up even by the youth of today. The humiliation felt led to a thorough, nationwide questioning of their own values. Chinese intellectuals and elites alike tried to make sense of why their nation, which had been the most powerful empire for centuries, suddenly found itself a victim. In their efforts to understand, Western texts were translated into Chinese. Within such a context, Western homophobia, paraded as Western science, started to infiltrate the Chinese consciousness. Finally, Britain imposed homophobic laws on the parts of China under its sovereignty, signalling the final death knell to the positive perception of homosexuality.

By the start of the twentieth century, homosexuality had been classified as a psychological disorder. Homophobia continued to grow in China as the century progressed. Under Mao, homosexuality in any form was banned and, during the Cultural Revolution, the persecution of gay people was sanctioned. Homosexuality became seen as Western 'spiritual pollution'. Mao destroyed vast swathes of the texts and public records of China's homosexual past. The nation forgot that it ever had a more liberal history.

Attitudes started to change under Deng Xiaoping. While he was no more of an advocate of homosexuality than Mao, articulation of a plurality of voices was more accepted and with that, the notion of homosexuality as an illness started to be challenged. For example, in 1985 a popular Chinese health magazine published an article expressing the view that homosexuals exist in all cultures and countries and that they should not be discriminated against. Sixty readers responded to the article, mostly gay men, describing the difficulties and despair that they faced on a daily basis as a result of living in China with their secret.

The biggest landmark was the decriminalisation of homosexuality in 1997. Another victory came four years later when homosexuality was removed from the list of mental illnesses. How far the nation had progressed was seen in 2005 at Fudan University, China's third-largest university, situated in Shanghai, when a course was introduced on gay and lesbian studies. It was so popular that students even sat on the floor. Shanghai also hosted China's first-ever Gay Pride event in 2009.

With this, civil society organisations for gay rights have not only strengthened, they have multiplied. A plethora of big organisations have been dealing with the issues and articulating important messages to the population at large. Even in terms of the lexicon, the favourable shift in attitude can be seen. The term *tongzhi* has arisen as the most popular contemporary Chinese word for LGBT people. The word has very positive historical references, originally being a Chinese translation from the Soviet Communist term 'comrade'. It was appropriated by a Hong Kong gay activist in 1989 for the first Lesbian and Gay Film Festival in Hong Kong who wanted to employ a more indigenous representation of same-sex eroticism. The term 'homosexual' was deemed inappropriate due to its use as a medical term denoting sickness and pathology at the time. Within a few years, *tongzhi* became widely used in Hong Kong and Taiwan, and then spread to China. As the term's roots imply, it has meaning beyond just being a sexual classification and legitimisation of same-sex love. It embodies a strong sentiment for integrating the sexual with the political (sharing the goals of fighting heterosexism) and with the cultural (reappropriating their Chinese identity).

More frank and open conversations about homosexuality have led to more reporting on the LGBT movement in the Chinese media. Before, dialogue in the 1990s and early 2000s was mostly concentrated on AIDS and how that affected the gay community. In recent years the balance has shifted to talk about non-health issues.

Like many aspects of China, progress appears to have come very quickly. But again, like many other aspects of China, these great headline statistics conceal more alarming truths. Saying that China is doing well in terms of its treatment of homosexuality would be to sugar-coat a very complex issue. Laws to protect homosexuals are still lacking, several Gay

Pride marches have been banned and the parade section of the 2009 Shanghai event was cancelled. And, while there are many positive stories in the Chinese press about being gay, such as features on gay marriages taking place (unofficial for now), there are other more prejudiced stories. One of my first baptisms of fire at the Chinese newspaper happened when I edited a story for World AIDS Day. The first line of the story read as follows: 'Wang was an ordinary art teacher until he started hanging out with a group of gays. Now he has AIDs.'

I had a long talk with the writer in question, who seemed confused about what was so wrong with the sentence. My other Chinese co-worker also failed to decipher why its assumed cause and effect was inaccurate and hurtful. Other colleagues laughed that the two people in question were 'anti-women, anti-Japanese and anti-gay' but it's no laughing matter and all three sentiments go unchallenged too often in present-day China.

It's unsurprising, given that as late as 2007 a survey conducted by sexologist Li Yinhe revealed that only 20 per cent of Chinese people believe there is nothing wrong with homosexuality, leaving the bulk of China still at odds with it. It's almost the reverse in the US, where a 2013 poll revealed that just 37 per cent believe it's a sin.

I speak to Stephen Leonelli, who was director of Beijing's LGBT centre from August 2012 to August 2013. Leonelli says there is still a lot of ignorance about homosexuality. Despite changes in legislation, people continue to treat it as an illness. Numerous textbooks are circulated in Chinese high schools describing gay people as 'perverts', so China's current graduates are growing up none the wiser. Leonelli lists a few other things from his experience that are not helping the achievement of universal rights for gay people. Psychologists, for example, advertise that they can make people straight again. Leonelli believes that, as a result of these messages, the average person on the street would say a gay person is sick and can be cured. For decades, all across the country, schemes have run which offer services that can 'cure' homosexuals. Elsewhere in the world, therapies claiming they can turn gay people straight have largely been discredited. No such outcry has taken place in China.

Homophobia in twenty-first-century China has also taken another turn. Just as in previous centuries, the family still looms large and parents want grandchildren as much as they always have, except now as a result of China's One Child Policy the pressure to procreate rests on the shoulders of fewer children. As mentioned earlier, there have been relaxations to the policy, allowing a couple to have two children if one of the partners is an only child. Yet many urban Chinese have said they have no desire to have more than one child, even though they now can. The surging cost of living has made small families much more appealing. For China's homosexual children, pressure to conform to a heteronormative role shows no sign of easing. A common joke circulates in gay communities: it is not about 'coming out' but 'coming home'.

Leonelli says,

> The discrimination and oppression of sexual minorities is very hidden in China. In the West we talk about violence or people being fired from their jobs e.g. very direct discrimination. In China it is more a case of individuals feeling that they have to hide their identity. Homo bashing is less heard of. It's more pressure from family and classmates.
>
> It touches on the greater issue of diversity. In China there is pressure to conform. Even the family members of someone who is gay will be pressurised. The whole structure of society is heterosexual. You have to get married and have a child. So when someone breaks from that mould, it is not very well-received.

With family being at the centre of issues gay people encounter, many gay people end up getting married. Some conceal their identity from their spouse, marrying a heterosexual person and masquerading as heterosexual. Li Yinhe, the sexologist, estimated in 2007 that approximately 80 per cent of gay men and women in China would marry. Others put the number higher. Their estimates aren't far off the mark: in today's China, stories of gay people being married and the negative side effects of this continue to circulate. For example, in June 2013, a woman named Hong Lingcong jumped to her death from a building after her husband admitted to her on microblogging platform Weibo that he was gay. This case ignited heated debate within the gay community regarding marriage, as many gay men and lesbian women still end up in loveless heterosexual marriages in order to please their families.

Unsurprisingly, within these kinds of relationships, infidelity is rife. One close friend in Beijing had direct experience of this. He had an affair with the secret gay lover of a very wealthy businessman. The businessman was married with kids, and he (the businessman) also owned an apartment in the centre of town where he paid for and kept another long-term gay lover as well as my friend's lover.

'It was a bit of a love nest and I used to invade every now and again,' he tells me.

The long-term lover and the businessman had been seeing each other for nearly ten years. The businessman paid for the apartment and gave his lover money regularly, under the proviso that he went along with being kept hidden away. All parties involved in this liaison were cheating on each other. The businessman specifically had other apartments across town set up as love dens. And all of this happened without the businessman's wife knowing anything about of it – a network of misters (as opposed to mistresses) in funded apartments all over town and a wife who was oblivious.

'When I realised the scale of this situation I stopped seeing the gay lover. I felt that this was a very risky sexual dynamic they were all engaged in, and even though I'd only been safe, I found it distasteful,' my friend adds.

The truth is that Chinese men might not be completely out of the closet, but providing that on the surface they play by the rules Chinese society dictates, they are free to do a lot beneath it. Cases of marriages of convenience between gay men and lesbians illustrate this. While I have personally never met anyone who has done this, I have heard it is a growing phenomenon in modern China. Leonelli says that of those who have entered this form of matrimony, approximately 50 per cent have come out to their parents.

'It's not all about concealment but about performance. It shows how complicated the structure of marriage is to Chinese society,' Leonelli summarises the growing gap between rhetoric and reality in China today. Chinese youth and sexual cultures are evolving faster than the country they are in. The question is: will China's social mores be able to catch up?

LEADING A DOUBLE LIFE: THE MEN WHO WON'T COME OUT TO THEIR FAMILIES

Dewei would never consider marrying a woman to keep up the pretence of being straight, and yet he is still cautious about who he reveals his sexuality to and who he doesn't. His parents fall into the second category. Dewei's justification for this casts light on the pressure placed on China's only children to conform to a heterosexual ideal.

I have met Dewei many times, one of the first being at the club Destination. He has a very sunny disposition and is always warm, welcoming and chatty. If anything, he is an over-sharer, which makes it all the more interesting that he is still in the closet with many people. One day we sit down and discuss why this is.

Dewei has a very good job at a top TV broadcaster. He is leading an independent, affluent life in Beijing and earns far more money than anyone else in the family, which he says does not actually amount to much as he comes from an impoverished background. Dewei was raised in Jiangxi Province, in south-east China, which is known to be one of the poorest provinces, especially compared to its neighbours; it is close to Shanghai and borders some of the country's wealthiest regions. When Dewei was around five years old, the economy was so bad in the province that his parents were forced to find work elsewhere. Like other children in 1980s China, he was raised by older relatives. From his descriptions, his house had a revolving door of family members. His grandma was one of nine and her sister moved in for a bit too. In another instance it was just him and his granddad.

'Neither of us knew how to do housework, so we just tried to make it work, learning how to wash socks etc. It's kinda sweet looking back actually,' he says, and I imagine a sweet double act of the blind leading the blind.

This situation ended when he went to a boarding school for his secondary education. It was one of the best schools in the region and he was thrilled when he got in. In his province in the 1990s boarding schools were quite a new phenomenon. Since then they have become more prolific and represent a growing trend in today's China, particularly for children from China's poorer and more rural areas. While the economic and social development of these rural regions has been remarkable, China's coastal cities are racing ahead at an even faster pace. This has fuelled an endless stream of people moving to the cities, in particular parents looking for work, who often leave children behind. Providing an education for children in less affluent areas has been one of China's major challenges, not least because the schools in these areas usually lag far behind their urban counterparts. Boarding schools have been one of the answers. Large numbers of small rural schools have been consolidated into a smaller number of big schools which benefit from a critical mass of teachers and services. These schools are often of a very high standard in terms of education. Many stand up well on an international level, which is all the more impressive given that the parents of the children who attend probably had little or no formal education. The schools are by no means luxurious, however. Accommodation is provided largely out of necessity as plenty of the students live too far away to commute on a daily basis. Dorms are often cramped, facilities basic and food the same.

This signifies an important break from non-Chinese boarding schools. Whereas boarding schools in the West usually suggest privilege, the cachet of boarding schools in China comes much more from exam results, not a sense of entitlement. Hence China's rich families still favour sending their children to boarding schools overseas or international schools in China over their own home-grown boarding schools.

It is becoming increasingly popular to send children as young as three to boarding school. The reasons are not simply about parents being unable to look after their children themselves or the school being too far away. Some parents think it is good for the children because it helps promote independence; they fear that, given the One Child Policy, a home dynamic of four grandparents, two parents and just one child could lead to the kid becoming very spoilt.

Dewei himself benefited from the excellent academic standard of his school, and the sense of independence has helped him deal with keeping the secret of his sexuality from his parents. 'I was very independent from an early age both mentally and physically. When I found out I was gay I didn't panic or feel the need to tell my family,' he says.

Dewei first became aware that he was gay aged 15 when he started visiting internet cafés. Pornography is illegal in China. It's considered moral pollution. Despite this it is readily available, mostly if you have access to a virtual private network (VPN), though also through other loopholes. According to Dewei, there were plenty of loopholes, even years ago.

He chanced upon gay porn. 'And that's how I found out about this fact!' he exclaims with a sense of pride, inflecting the words upwards at the end to suggest it was a welcome surprise, or at least one that he has come to terms with.

Dewei didn't act on the newfound information for some time. His high-school years were typical of those of any Chinese kid, defined by hard work and not much else. A love life was very much at the back of his mind, until the last year of school when a cute guy was transferred from another school, whom Dewei described as his first proper crush (just a crush; the guy was heterosexual and had a girlfriend).

He told no one at school that he was gay and continued to keep it a secret at college. It was only later that he started identifying more openly as gay, specifically upon losing his virginity. He was 21 and had never even kissed, let alone had sex. There were no gay clubs affiliated with his university and Tianjin, the city where his university was, housed no gay clubs at all to his knowledge.

'At that stage I was so in the closet, I was buried in it! Also I studied very hard, all day. And I was into video games in the second and third years. I would play at least two hours a night.'

Nonetheless it was in Tianjin that he did have his first sexual encounter, meeting a lover online. 'It's like Pandora's Box – once you open it, things keep coming out!' he says, chuckling away.

Since opening Pandora's Box, Dewei has acquired a preference for dates instead of hook-ups, he's keen to stress. Hook-ups are easy to come by in Beijing. The geo-navigation-enabled apps Grindr and Jack'd are huge in the city, both of them promoting a culture of easy sex.

By the time we meet, Dewei is out to a few classmates from university, a few colleagues and most of his Beijing friends, many of whom he has met through the gay scene. But his family still do not know and he would like to keep it that way.

'I think it will be really ugly if I tell them because they are from the countryside. They're very traditional. I am meant to continue the family line. My father only has me, so basically the branch of my father's family will stop if I don't have a child.'

Both his dad and grandparents want him to have children, while his mother places pressure on him to have a normal, settled life. Initially this involved getting a good job.

'Until I was done with my studies and had secured a good job [at China's leading TV station], my mum would always end conversations with "Don't date, concentrate on work." Once I got a job it changed to, "Are you dating anyone?"' It's a line I hear a lot, mostly from the women I have spoken to.

Dewei deflects his mother's questions by telling her he is working hard and that everyone at his company is older and already married. The reality is actually the opposite; Dewei's office is an ideal place to meet someone for those who are looking. State corporations encourage people to date internally, which makes sense given that it is the state that often spearheads campaigns to get people coupled up. Dewei's work specifically holds matchmaking events for singles annually. They invite people from similar organisations, such as a recent event attended by singles from China's national radio service.

Still, Dewei's mother continues to ask her son when he will bring home a girl.

'What's holding you back [from telling her]?' I ask. He says his mother's life has been marred by hardship and tragedy. She has spent years working hard on a factory floor and also found out that her husband, Dewei's father, has been having an affair; his work demanded a lot of time outside the factory, going to work dinners and the like. In China, work is never just work, as Dewei's story reminds me. Dewei's mother followed him one day and discovered that he had a mistress, whom he had put up in an apartment.

His mother felt hopeless in the situation, feeling that a divorce would place her in a weaker position than staying together. On top of prejudice against divorcees, which remains acute in China's less-affluent and rural areas, Dewei's mother is a victim to the aforementioned law regarding residential property rights in China. The home she shares with Dewei's father is in his name, not hers, meaning she is entitled to nothing in the event of a separation, and she didn't have much to start with.

'So my mum has had a hard time and the only thing she's proud of is me,' he says, suddenly looking very sad. 'You know, she was such a great beauty back in the day,' he adds wistfully.

Dewei is not sure his mother could handle his sexual orientation and the area Dewei was raised in makes matters worse.

I'm from a small town and people gossip. I'm the first one from my town to get into the central government. When I go back all the villagers point and say 'Oh, it's that kid in TV.' Mum's quite proud of that. So if I come out to them, people in the village will talk about it. All of the good stuff won't matter to those people.

Dewei's story highlights an interesting point. While the gap between China's rural and urban areas is huge and growing, the two are still connected. Dewei might be living in the city now, but he is from the countryside. Youth such as Dewei feel the impact of tensions between rural and urban life the most, and in that respect between tradition and modernity in China. He says his mother does not even know that he goes clubbing, nor would she properly understand. His lifestyle and sexual choices are simply beyond her reference points.

And yet even in Beijing, where attitudes are as progressive as they come in China, Dewei still experiences homophobia. It's not of an everyday variety. Dewei points to his clothes and I look him up and down. He is clad in Converse, jeans and a hoodie, looking like a typical emo kid. 'I don't look gay right? No one knows on the street.'

Still, there have been two instances recently which have shaken him. One occurred at the end of a date. He was hailing a cab with the man. It was quite late and when the cab stopped, Dewei kissed his date on the cheek to say goodbye. The taxi driver drove off. When the next one pulled up, they didn't embrace and had no issue.

In another instance, he was eating lunch with his work team, which was mostly women. They were talking about gay people and for the most part it was positive, albeit generalised. Then one said, 'If my son doesn't bring home a man, I will consider it a good thing.' Dewei's perception is that their level of acceptance is higher towards those who are a bit more distant, as opposed to an immediate relative. This attitude isn't far removed from the attitude many urban residents of the US and UK express when they say they would find it 'easier' if their children were not gay. To argue that the West is fully accepting of gay relationships is to gloss over the deep prejudices still held by many. However, as with plenty of things in China, the One Child family changes the dynamics. And whereas in the UK and US discrimination is being confronted head-on (I recently witnessed my first legal gay marriage in London to roars of support), in China the legal infrastructure only supports heterosexual couples, and only really men at that.

That Dewei is not out to everyone is hardly surprising. He is from a poor, rural background and works in state media where the messages can be very conservative. What about those who operate on the more liberal end of Chinese society?

Zong also has a conflicted relationship with his sexuality. When I meet him he appears very self-assured and cuts a fashionable shape. The 26-year-old is dressed in tailored grey tartan trousers, a black military-style top and shiny brogues (English, handmade, I am soon told). I meet him at the gallery he is working at in the 798 Art Zone.

Beijing has many different art villages and hubs, with 798 being the original. 798 is in the area formerly known as the Dashanzi factory complex. It was originally a steel production area, which officially began production in 1957. It was made up of several *danwei* – work units – each offering considerable social benefits to its 10,000-plus inhabitants, and fully furnished rooms to whole families at minimal cost. After the death of Mao, the factory area lay derelict until artists started to occupy it and use the space for their studios. Over the past ten years it has become incredibly commercial and is a lively hub of galleries, shops and cafés. It continues to exercise a lot of commercial muscle, while other artist villages have sprung up in more far-flung places to cater for more underground artists or those who want to be perceived as such – like Ai Weiwei, whose studio is in Caochangdi, the second-biggest art village.

I meet Zong at his gallery, where he gives me a private tour. The huge wealth China is generating is hanging from the walls in the form of art worth millions of yuan. After the tour we head outside and grab a drink on the main promenade. Zong starts by telling me:

I have two very good friends who are so Christian. One holds my hand and says, 'I am so sorry that you are gay.' She goes to Israel every year. She's the owner of a top designer store in Shanghai. I also know one girl who converted to Judaism because she wants to marry a Jewish guy. She thinks they're all really rich!

Zong is from Chongqing, Sichuan Province, and describes himself as upper middle class, clearly both hyper-aware of the UK class distinctions and displaying how class is really becoming important in contemporary China. His parents are middle-level officials in local government and, while he does not classify himself as super-rich, he is certainly not poor and hangs out with plenty of the elite. It's the central irony of modern China: the route to riches is through the party which originally set out to redistribute them.

Zong's childhood was interesting, to say the least. When he was around the age of four, his grandmother, who had been taking care of him so his parents could go to work, passed away. They couldn't find anyone to replace her so his parents sent him to one of the special Beijing Olympic preparation schools which had just opened in the area.

Basically the Chinese government was obsessed with the Olympics and they were training kids from a very early age. I was trained as a diver. But it was so brutal and my father stopped it. I had to learn to swim. They put all of the kids into a swimming pool and left us to drown. I had only been there two weeks when my father saw it. It was just so inhuman!

He [father] asked for me to be moved to gymnastics. I was there from seven until middle school and that is why I am so flexible and have done ballet!

Zong says, and holds out his arms as if he is a circus magician.
He went to the Olympic academy until the age of 11 and then transferred to a local school. After high school he enrolled at a

small business school in Shanghai and later found his calling at a gallery in Shanghai. He then applied for an MA in Art in the US and ended up in New York. He stayed there for a couple of years and was lured back to China on being offered a good job at a top gallery in Shanghai. 'I was so enjoying being a hipster, living in Brooklyn, and then a major art dealer found me and asked me to come home. I worked in Shanghai for her for a year and then made the move to Beijing six months ago.'

Zong quickly gives me an overview of Chinese art in 60 seconds, all from his perspective. Chinese contemporary art is booming, but compared to most of Europe, Central America and the US it is not so contemporary. It took off after Mao. The first generation painted cynical realism and political pop. It was internal orientalism and was very much done for Westerners. This generation mostly left after the Tiananmen Square incident of 1989.

By comparison, the second generation rarely left China. They liked the country and enjoyed the rising quality of life there. Finally, there's the third generation, who are the One Child generation. This group fragments into the haves and the have-nots; those who are from the grassroots and those who are rich. Zong mentions one successful artist in this group as an example.

He is gay, a big diva and from my hometown. We both know each other but we don't like each other. His mum sells vegetables. Ha! But he knows how to promote himself, even though his work is a joke. He's basically the Chinese version of Andy Warhol. He slept around to get famous. That's very Chinese. For success they will do anything. But I don't do that. I believe in principles.

Zong declares, crossing his arms and shaking his head.

The third generation, who are growing in number as art becomes an increasingly well-respected profession for China's youth, are not radical enough for Zong: 'I share some mentality with them but deep in my heart I have an anti-establishment mentality. I am like "fuck you". I'm so enjoying the subcultures like Brooklyn and the East End of London.'

Zong is confident and very direct. He is also part of a very international, jet-setting crowd. And yet despite all of this, he is still hiding his sexuality from his parents. It shows just how deep-seated these prejudices are.

Zong reckons deep down they know.

'My parents pretend they don't know that I am gay. I was using Chanel lipstick one time at home and my mum asked me why I was not wearing Max Factor. I was like, Mum why aren't you asking me whether I am gay?'

'So why don't you tell her?' I ask.

'I can't tell her. I can't,' he says. 'No. She wouldn't accept it. For three generations I am the only son. I can't tell them.' He banishes the idea with a violent shake of the head.

'How is your love life then?' I ask, shifting the direction of the conversation.

'Urgh, my love life is not going well because I intimidate a lot of people,' he explains and it is easy to understand how he has come to that conclusion. 'So I'm dating lots of older guys. I prefer northern European hipster types. In fact, I don't date Chinese at all. Also my mindset is quite Western,' he adds, flicking his head to the side as if he has long locks. In the middle of another swing, as he starts to launch into the next sentence, his phone goes.

'I'm sorry, darling, my friend is now in 798. I must dash,' he announces and with that quickly throws cash onto the table for the drink, kisses me on both cheeks – a very European affectation – and runs back in the direction of his studio.

AN ALMOST OUT AND PROUD MINORITY

Not all gay people in China conceal their sexuality. There are those who have come out and are living their lives in an open manner. In 2012 the documentary *Mama Rainbow* aired. It showed mothers of gay men stepping forward to say they were embracing their sons' sexuality. Weiwei's mother was ahead of the trend. She stepped forward a long time ago.

Like Zong, Weiwei is not your typical Chinese, he tells me, though really words are not necessary. From his perfect, articulated English and his BA from Stanford, it is clear that the suave man in front of me is not representative of an average gay person's experience in China. Weiwei, who is in his thirties, grew up in a town three hours away from Harbin, the north-eastern city close to the Russian border that was famous for its winter ice festival (think mini Great Walls and fairytale castles). He is the son of two artists and describes himself as always being confident and able to explore non-conventional paths. His mother is a ballerina and his father a musician. They were young when they had him and he describes his upbringing as very liberal and open-minded. As a result, he felt comfortable coming out to them, which he did aged 18, and they have always been accepting.

A few months later he went to university, attending Beida, one of Beijing's top universities, which is known as the one to go to if you wanted to study the arts.

'But I dropped out because it's a horrible school. It's meant to be the most liberal school in the country, a place to create poets. It's not like that at all. It's very mind controlling,' he explains.

He managed just a term there before leaving. It was during that first term that he met his boyfriend and the pair have been together ever since.

Weiwei describes his boyfriend as pretty closed, although in this case 'closed' is relative. Weiwei is out to everyone. His boyfriend, on the other hand, is more guarded about who he comes out to. He has come out to his mother, who refused to let him tell his father; she thinks it is a phase and doesn't want to acknowledge it. Even though the pair have been living together for over a decade, the mother still treats it like a dirty secret. The father, meanwhile, believes they are just roommates, which is a common line that gay men and women in China employ.

There is another unusual twist in Weiwei's story – he is a father. Weiwei runs a foundation in China which works with impoverished children. As a result of his work there he was able to adopt (otherwise it would have been very hard for a single man to do so).

'I work in orphanages and it was love at first sight with a one-and-a-half-year-old [his daughter].'

She's now four and knows she has two fathers. She lives most of the time with the grandmother (Weiwei's mother) back up in Harbin and Weiwei tries to see her as much as possible. He is going back up north for a few weeks after we meet, and you can see the excitement in his eyes as he speaks of his daughter.

Another person who has revealed her true sexuality to her parents is Shane, as she likes to be referred to. Shane, who is a teacher, describes herself as a tomboy. Upon gaining self-awareness, she was not into having long hair or wearing skirts, unlike the other girls at school, and this was one of the first signs that made her realise she was a lesbian.

'Of course when I was three years old I didn't know that I was a lesbian. However, I always liked to play with pretty girls,' she tells me. It was later on that the penny dropped.

'When I started university I was exposed to more information and I began to define my orientation. It wasn't a complicated process. It was just that things I had always been doing took on a different definition, and I became happy.'

She then came out to her parents, who were not shocked at all.

'Because of the way I dressed my parents were already used to the idea. That said, my mother still wishes the situation would change. My father has given us his blessing.'

By us, Shane is referring to herself and her girlfriend from university, whom she met just before she left. She said that for years she held on to a romantic conception of love, wanting to find someone to spend an eternity with. When she met no one, she started to become disillusioned. Then love walked into her life.

'We have now been together for six years, and I feel extremely lucky. It's no longer a relationship of great passion, but it is still very sweet and loving,' she confides.

THE L WORD

Shane, who refers to herself by the ubiquitous term 'Lala', lifted from a 1994 Taiwanese novel *Notes of a Crocodile*, which features a lesbian of the same name, has a largely positive experience of being a lesbian in China.

'These days China is pretty good. Chinese people have quite a moderate attitude, and there is not a huge amount of animosity,' she notes, adding that heterosexuals do not generally discriminate in public, and that she has not experienced any discrimination herself. For this reason she's keen to fight for those who are not yet openly gay. As for marriages of convenience, she believes they're wrong.

But for all of her bravery, Shane is still not out with everyone.

'My boss does not know – in China you still have to be cautious about coming out in a work environment, unless you are in a very tolerant industry, like the entertainment industry, for example. Government workers and teachers etc. for the most part don't come out at work.'

Is it easy for lesbians to meet, I ask Shane? The few gay clubs that I know of in Beijing largely cater to a male crowd, so I wonder what the options are like for lesbians. Shane confirms my suspicions that the city is more friendly for gay men than for gay women. Nonetheless she is upbeat.

'If I look around me at my immediate friends, I would say that it is not so hard. These days there are a lot of web platforms where you can meet people, or there is one venue you can go to.'

Shane is coming of age at an interesting moment. Change has been slower for gay women. This mirrors a historical pattern: in China lesbians have always been more marginalised. Most literary references of same-sex relationships are boy with boy. Mentions of female love are usually favourable. For example, the famous novel *Dream of the Red Chamber* by Cao Xueqin, from the middle of the eighteenth century, narrates the story of two actresses who fall in love, to the acceptance of the book's protagonist. Yet until 2005 – noted as the year that the growth of lesbian groups started to become visible – their voices were still muffled. Resources within the homosexual community were mostly directed towards tackling AIDS and other major health concerns. In this, lesbian issues were overlooked.

Chinese lesbians often also suffer their own unique form of homophobia. On top of the pressures to conform to the heteronormative model and produce children are other pressures. Once again, China's skewed gender ratio with its excess of men means that many single Chinese men are resentful of any reduction in the pool of potential wives. Lesbians have been known to bear the brunt of this resentment. They also suffer from an amplification of the prejudice that all women face in China – a partnership of two women face the dual burden of chauvinism and homophobia. Gay men in China have even been known to discriminate against lesbians. It is not always the case that they are all in it together.

Fortunately, the LGBT movement has started to concentrate more on rights, alongside health issues, which has had a positive knock-on effect for lesbians. In addition, lesbian groups are now aligning themselves with female rights groups. While still far from prominent, as the chapter on feminism discusses below, these groups have been strengthened and are pushing for a concentration on the discrimination all women face. Shane describes her life as charmed and the hope is that her experience can spread to other homosexual women across China.

THE BIGGEST BATTLEGROUND: TRANS IN CHINA

Where change is most stubborn is with transgendered and transsexual people. China actually has a long history of cross-dressing. There are many instances in Chinese history in which a third gender or variations on a gender are notable – the eunuchs living in the Forbidden City being the most obvious example. In another instance, when Manchurian women did not bind their feet in the early Qing Dynasty, they were seen as masculine compared to Chinese women with bound feet. Chinese men were not attracted to 'large-footed' Manchurian women, as the small bound foot was seen as a gender marker. Feminine men also played women on stage in Peking Opera, even living as women, as noted in the semi-fictionalised *M. Butterfly*, which is based on the affair between French diplomat Bernard Boursicot and Chinese opera singer Shi Pei Pu, who posed as a woman.

In the present, the transgendered community also benefit from having a poster girl in the form of Jin Xing, a professional dancer who currently lives in Shanghai. By contrast, there are no openly gay politicians, nor are there openly gay celebrities in the more accepting realms of showbiz. The common theme of family and harmony means that in some instances transgendered individuals are more socially accepted in China than gay men and women. If someone undergoes a sex change and then engages in a regular relationship, they are less of a visible threat to the system.

Despite these examples, trans issues have rarely been confronted. In 2012 a study was conducted that showed non-conforming youth were more subject to bullying. This was the same year that Dasige, a prominent transgendered individual in Dalian, had his house set on fire. Transgender is still listed as a mental disorder and gender reassignment remains taboo. A 2010 report from the International Gay and Lesbian Human Rights Commission on China describes the ways in which prejudice is manifested: 'Transgendered people face serious levels of police harassment in China. The transgendered community also faces particular difficulties in obtaining employment. The Chinese authorities are currently consulting on new rules on gender realignment surgery. In certain aspects these rules fail to meet international standards on individual autonomy and privacy.'

Gender reassignment surgery has been available in China since the 1980s, but numbers of recorded procedures remain low. This is in part because government-implemented guidelines in 2009 have restricted the number of people eligible for gender reassignment surgery. According to the guidelines, a person is required to apply with the police to change the gender on their official registration before undergoing gender reassignment surgery, and to have the consent of their parents. They must have lived openly as the gender with which they identify for a number of years before the surgery. In addition, they cannot have a criminal record, must be 20 years or over and unmarried. They have to undergo therapy and have a psychiatric test to prove they have gender dysmorphia. There are other restrictions making it beyond the reach of many. For example, they can only change their gender officially if they have full surgery, which is something that simply does not fit all identities. Even for those who wish to have the full surgery, the aftermath is not straightforward. Academic records and urban residency (*hukou*) are documented under name and gender of birth, so people lose these in the process, which places them in a severely compromised position given the importance of these two documents in Chinese society. And none of this says anything of the price of the surgery.

'For those from a lower-income bracket in particular, these are a lot of hurdles. It's a very troublesome process,' Stephen Leonelli from Beijing's LGBT centre notes when we discuss the trans community.

Han Bingbing, a Chinese woman who underwent gender reassignment surgery in 1999, commented on the 2009 guidelines in an interview with *China Daily*:

> I would not be able to have the surgery if there was such a guideline in 1999 [...] my mother died when I was seven and I was not able to speak to my father about my feelings until I returned to my hometown after the operation. He was outraged and heartbroken. Even now I can see how sad it still makes him. Most transsexuals are not on good terms with their family. That is the reality. They sometimes change their names and move far away. What happens if their family refuses to let them have the surgery?

In spite of restrictive regulations, the past few years have nevertheless witnessed a few positive signs of change. In

2012, for example, an 84-year-old Foshan woman and former government official named Qian Jinfan, who came out as transgendered at the age of 80, began to talk openly to the public about her experience. She told the government agency that paid her retirement benefits, and her wife, who were all tolerant and supportive. Qian said: 'At first, I prepared to defend myself whatever the cost, but then I found I had been accepted. Their tolerance towards transgenders went beyond the scope of my imagination.'

Meanwhile, news of the love affair between American transgendered teenagers Katie Hill and Arin Andrews received a largely positive reaction on Chinese social media in the summer of 2013, just months ahead of new Beijing band Nova Heart releasing a music video to their song 'Beautiful Boys', which followed the lives of transgendered sex workers.

A VULNERABLE MINORITY:
STI WITHIN THE LGBT COMMUNITY

The aforementioned lack of sex education is especially apparent in same-sex circles. Dewei notes that homosexual men in China are reluctant to use condoms. The majority of people he knows avoid protection altogether. He says he practises safe sex, but also stipulates that he is not very promiscuous, favouring long-term relationships. Dewei says that a friend of his who is more inclined towards random sexual encounters often faces resistance from lovers when he uses a condom.

'I think Asian gays are quite passive. They take the woman's role in bed as the receiver. The condom only really affects the feel of the giver,' he says.

A British gay friend of mine cuts straight to the point when asked of his experience of condom usage:

Contraception is a big issue in Beijing, and in China as a whole. It's not so much that guys were reluctant to use condoms, more that they were keen to have sex without them. In China, there isn't a full appreciation of the dangers of unsafe sex and HIV. Many students have almost no sex education at school, except from a purely biological point of view.

He narrates the story of a friend of his who ran a summer school in Beijing with the aim of educating the future leaders of China. Each summer he brought in a woman who worked in HIV prevention to lecture the children. He reported that she had said, 'Your kids don't know what a penis is, don't know what a vagina is; that's wrong, you need to sort this out.' She was talking about students who are aged 14 to 16, very wealthy and very educated in Chinese terms – Beijing kids.

If Beijing kids have no clue about safe sex then what clue do the kids from the provinces have? If straight kids have no clue about straight safe sex, then what clue is there about gay safe sex? The sex education policy seems to be, you're too young to have sex, so don't have sex, you'll be old enough when you graduate from your masters. But, inevitably closer relationships and curious minds lead to experimentation and that leads to college students putting themselves in danger.

Perhaps the trend is changing, though, the British friend adds: 'One former lover recently tested negative and other friends have been posting pictures of the results of their oral home HIV tests onto Weixin [a social media platform]. Of course, only the ones who test negative do this.'

While some are trying their hardest to educate the gay community about safe sex, the government is tackling the problem in less effective ways – for example, by jamming the incredibly popular gay hook-up apps Grindr and Jack'd. By the end of 2013 the two sites were hardly working on 3G or mobile internet, only on wi-fi or with a VPN. The rationale is that if it cracks down on hook-up software it will reduce HIV transmission, except that people will always find ways to hook up, so its efforts are ineffectual and a waste of resources and energy which could be otherwise directed at campaigns that actually raise awareness.

It would be wrong to conclude that the Chinese LGBT world is undergoing a revolution but, all things considered, it is certainly undergoing an evolution. Prior to the passage of gay marriage laws in several US states, there was speculation on whether gay marriage would arrive in China ahead of America. This was optimistic. Although government policy on homosexuality is being relaxed, marriage is a long way off at present. What does stand to reason is that small steps continue to make a big difference. Even the people interviewed here who are not out to everyone are not being completely dishonest to themselves. Rather, concealment is just one of many strategies they are choosing to deal with changing realities in China. Maybe in the future the pendulum will swing a different way and the pressure to conform to a traditional dynamic will not be as intense. In the meantime, between bars and social networks, online and off, the visibility of the LGBT community has significantly increased and none of the interviewees felt isolated. This is an accomplishment in modern, urban China, where even friendships, let alone relationships, are proving increasingly difficult to foster.

9

China's Pussy Riot

All the problems in China are created by men.
Gia W, the queen of Chinese punk

China did not experience the feminist awakening that America and Europe did in the 1960s and 1970s. After Chairman Mao's pledge that women would hold up half the sky, they started to dress more like men and fill roles previously assigned to men, challenging certain stereotypes, but women did not tackle deep-seated gender bias.

This started to change from the 1980s, when books on gender theory were translated into Chinese and China saw its first 'wave' of feminist scholarship. Feminism remained within academic borders for the next few decades. Then in the 2000s it gained momentum at a social level. Women started to acquire a voice, and stories began to appear about guerrilla feminism, so to speak – women spontaneously taking action to highlight a certain cause. For example, in the summer of 2012 two women draped in black robes took to the Shanghai subway in protest. They wore placards that read, 'I can be flirtatious, but you can't harass' and 'We want to feel cool! We don't want dirty hands.' The photos were a reaction to a sign on Shanghai Metro's microblog which said, 'Girls, please be self-dignified to avoid perverts' – the state's clumsy response to a rise in sexual harassment on the subway.

In recent years, these stories are becoming more frequent and are very encouraging. Even if China does not have many groups dedicated to strengthening women, it is no longer lacking individuals fighting for the cause. Amongst the most notorious is Wang Yue or, to use her stage name, Gia, a rock star who could be labelled the Chinese version of Pussy Riot.

Gia's story is remarkable and sums up all of the extremes and contradictions of being young and female in China. She first encountered fame as the vocalist in the Chinese all-female rock band Hang on the Box (HOTB), which was formed in 1998 when she and her friends were only 15 years old. Gia revels in the accolade of being the front woman of China's first all-girl punk group, a remarkable feat in any context, let alone in China.

In Jonathan Campbell's detailed book on the advent of Chinese rock music, *Red Rock: The Long, Strange March of Chinese Rock and Roll*, he recounts Wang and band member Yilina's punk conversion. 'Their lives were changed the moment they saw their first show,' Campbell writes. 'The Mohawks, the dyed hair, the sunglasses (inside!); they'd never seen anything like it.' Wang told Campbell, 'You didn't know what made [the punks] special but you knew that, in comparison, you were a jackass. [...] I called Yilina and said, "Our entire life before was completely stupid. We need to become like them: our taste in music, our attitude, our lives."'

The band is a phenomenal success, both within China and beyond. The road has not always been straight and smooth, of course. It featured a first live performance to a chorus of boos and mockery, countless break-ups and reconciliations and a constant struggle to secure gigs, record deals and respect.

But HOTB were a sensation. Within just six months of their first live gig, they appeared on the cover of a Chinese edition of *Newsweek*, serving as poster girls for an entire generation of Chinese youth. In 2004 and 2005, HOTB was nominated for the Best Rock Band gong at the Chinese equivalent of the Grammy Music Awards, the Annual Pepsi Music Awards. They also quickly acquired cult status in Japan and the United States. Unlike most other Chinese rock bands, HOTB have toured in these countries, as well as China and Hong Kong. They have a huge fan base, including celebrities such as Marilyn Manson, and have played at prominent international festivals like South by Southwest.

Their story is not only significant in terms of Chinese rock music; it is also a story of women carving out a voice in a predominantly patriarchal environment. HOTB have been lauded by critics for politicising gender through their empowered, femme-forward lyrics. *Yellow Banana*, their first album, which was released in 2001, featured riot grrrl-esque songs like 'Asshole, I'm Not Your Baby', 'No Sexy' and 'For Some Stupid Cunts at BBS'. Early material was littered with swear words, and the girls courted controversy. For example, when they did a photo shoot where they flaunted their underwear, members of the public asked them whether they were running a brothel.

Seeing women embrace their sexuality and speak in a way that was less demure was a first for China and made the band members targets of hate as much as admiration. The image most common for Chinese women at the time – and to this day – is that of the young, wide-eyed beauty from Japanese cartoons, and many Chinese girls infantilise themselves to fit the mould. The markets in China's shopping districts have plenty of stores selling clothes to adults that look more as if they are designed for children – dresses in pale blues and pinks with bows and ribbons on. Accompanying this fragile, childlike look is the affected *sa jiao*, 'cute whining', done in the fashion of a demanding child. Gia and her band members are the opposite of that. They wear bold colours, have piercings and tattoos. They speak with attitude and they shock people.

Gia sings about the issues that are important to women. 'Kill Your Belly' is reputedly about abortion, for example. It strikes a chord in a population where abortion is rife. And the issues that Gia has been singing about for the past two decades still matter now. Change is coming to Chinese women, but not fast enough – a central irony in a country defined by its bullet-fast change. Does this frustrate her? I arrange an interview with Gia, with the proviso that we do not talk about politics at all – a reasonable request in a country where artists aren't immune from the heavy hand of the government, as the 2011 arrest and imprisonment of Ai Weiwei highlights.

Gia's apartment is located in an unassuming complex in central Beijing. It's up several flights of concrete stairs in a block with no lift. I knock on the door. A moment later it swings open and Gia stands in front of me.

My first impression is that she is much smaller in life than I had assumed; perhaps the legend surrounding her had added stature in my mind. Then my eyes dart to her clothes. She is a fashion chameleon – and a fashion sensation. Throughout the years she has modelled as many different hairstyles as Madonna. The current one is a jagged bob and fringe with two streaks of pale pink contrasting the rich black. Complementing her hair is neon pink lipstick and black wet-look leggings. A bracelet reading 'No more Gia' and a T-shirt embellished with the word SEX across it catch the eye. The T-shirt is one of her own designs, she proudly tells me.

'It's not for any message. I just like the look of the letters together. I even considered SEXY but the Y doesn't look as good,' she explains.

Gia's living room is like her own style, a design of punk meets Barbie, with pink fluffy cushions – one of which has 'Gia' written on it – a large cross on the wall and a poster saying 'Have Punk'. Her cat, Bella, is lying languorously on one of the cushions, taking up a key position on the small sofa.

Gia's home is the opposite of many Chinese apartments I've been to, which can be gaudy in a 1980s sort of way, if design is given any attention. Typically aesthetics give way to pragmatism, and home furnishing stores are a rarity in China. For those in search of style, Ikea dominates and does not have to fight off competition from home-grown stores.

Gia asks what I want to drink and hurries into the back, soon to come out with a pot of loose-leaf chrysanthemum tea. She sits down and immediately dives into how she got into music, an anecdote which is the flip side of narratives about Chinese girls who study hard and settle down early, their paths dictated to them by convention.

'It's quite a funny story actually,' she says, as she nestles down on the couch, lifting Bella onto her knee. Gia first heard rock music when she was 13 and from the get-go loved it. At the time she described herself as a 'good girl'. She was head of the class for maths and was the class monitor. Ironically, it was through doing everything that she was told – through conforming – that she became a non-conformist. On one fateful day, a boy in her class was passing around a cassette tape. When the teacher caught wind of what was happening, she confiscated it, tearing up the piece of paper inside the box containing the song names and handing the ruins to Gia to dispose of. She was the wrong person to hand it to. Instead of binning it, she stuck the pieces of paper together and listened to the tape. It was called *Chinese Fire* and was a compendium of all of the hottest rock bands in China at the time. From that moment she became hooked on music. The idea of creating an all-female band soon dawned on her at a live music venue in Beijing.

Gia's music is all in English, in theory at least. The reality is more like a made-up language, as her command of English is basic. Sentence structures are peculiar. She tells me that in her early days she was dating a native English speaker who would read her work in advance. He didn't want to correct it because he believed it added an element of quirkiness, and there is no denying that. The result is often an indecipherable drawl of vaguely English sounds.

Even without confident English skills, singing in English was and still is a smart move for Chinese youth who want to challenge the status quo without attracting too much attention. English adds an air of intrigue to the songs; it also makes the artists less of a target for the government's censors, who are more likely to go after those whose messages can be understood beyond an intellectual niche.

What does Gia think about the music industry in China now?

Rock music in China is not really rock music. It has become really commercial. For a lot of young people in China values have changed. Back in the day a lot of rock music was anti-establishment. Now it is no longer this sacred thing that people pursue, but instead used as a vehicle for fame.

CHINESE GIRLS EYE UP THE WEST

Gia's scepticism about the direction the Chinese music industry is heading in has not stopped her from continuing to use music as a vehicle to vent frustrations about Chinese society. Like the songs she wrote a decade earlier, she is still articulating grievances felt by a sizable chunk of Chinese women.

Youth remain the primary target for Gia, with a few 'types' of youth particularly angering her. The country's supposed fashionistas, for example: 'There's this word in China – *zhongbi* – about girls who speak in Chinese but add a few English words into their sentences and pretend to have travelled abroad and have lots of foreign exposure. They take photos of themselves with wine glasses, for example.' She starts laughing and shaking her head.

The worst offenders are the girls who accessorise their lives with Western boyfriends, not just Western products. Her band's 2007 album, *No More Nice Girls*, contains the controversial song 'Shanghai'. Some of the verses in the song go as follows: 'What is Shanghai? Rich white cock and hungry yellow chick. What is Shanghai? Stupid white cock and hungry yellow chick.'

At the time of its release, people argued about its message. Was it trying to incite 'yellow fever', as the white, predominantly male fetishisation of Chinese women is often referred to in its most crude way? Or was it instead a sharp critique of author Wei Hui and the hype around her bestselling semi-autobiographical tale *Shanghai Baby*, in which the protagonist Nikki/Coco has an illicit affair with a BMW-driving German, Mark?

Years later Gia still mocks the girls who only want a Western boyfriend, 'the hungry yellow chicks' as she continues to call them.

I can see where her derision comes from. This is a feature of urban China. Beijing and Shanghai have been referred to as dating Meccas for the Western (white) male, and dating graveyards for the Western female. The logic runs that white men are sexually attracted to Chinese women, with their petite frames and almond eyes, and that Chinese women in turn look up to Western men as embodiments of masculinity. (As earlier noted, ideas of masculinity in China are complicated and dissimilar to Western notions. That said, there are areas of overlap, such as a preference for tall men.) The reverse operates for Chinese men and Western women. We are seen as too masculine and domineering, and Western women for the most part view Chinese men as too timid, effeminate and different – the cultural divide cited as insurmountable. The sense of 'other' that appeals to the Western male–Chinese female dynamic does not work well in reverse.

It's not just in terms of appearance that a Western man can appeal. In the 1990s and early 2000s in particular, when the Chinese economic miracle was only just underway, the Western male represented a means of escape from a hard life. Even a low-paid Western man was still on a decent salary compared to most Chinese. Western men could 'upgrade' in the Chinese love market – that is, have a more attractive Chinese girlfriend. Western girls didn't have as much cachet; their high salaries intimidated many Chinese men. And so a phrase came to dominate dating in Beijing, for those girls who were only willing to date Western guys: the odds aren't good but the goods are odd.

These dynamics are said to operate to this day. However, some distinctions must be made. Firstly, it is erroneous to think that all Chinese women were and are desperate for a Western boyfriend. I have spoken to plenty of Chinese girls who also believe the cultural gap is too big and who would prefer to date someone from their own country. Some also say their parents – perhaps educated in Maoist, Cold War-style rhetoric that cautioned against the West – have a distrust of white foreigners and would be displeased if their daughter brought one home. Gia's mother, for one, nearly fainted when she heard Gia was dating an Englishman, and referred to him as a foreign devil. It is therefore not the case that Westerners are always put on a pedestal in China. There is as much distrust and animosity as there is respect and adoration, with occasional flare-ups in the major expat cities, such as in 2012 when the leaked video of a

Western man molesting a Chinese woman in Beijing sparked retribution from the Chinese community.

Secondly, there has been a marked increase in the number of Western women dating Chinese men. Orientalism, a shallow reference to Edward Said's groundbreaking book about the Western creation of the 'Oriental other', is unravelling. There are probably a few reasons for this. More Western girls are taking time to learn about Chinese language and culture, which is bridging the cultural divide. And Chinese men, for their part, are wealthier, more confident and developing more gumption when it comes to Western girls, approaching them more than ever before. It is one of the greatest changes I have noticed between the China I first came to in 2006 and the China of now; it shows how the relationship between China and the West is being renegotiated.

'Back in the day Shanghai girls loved to find themselves a *laowai* [Chinese term given to foreigners]. Now *laowai* are less rich, so they don't want them as much!' says Gia on these changing dynamics and it's true – the hordes of English teachers that used to pick up Chinese girls easily are having a tougher time of it. Foreign men in China can no longer just fall back on their perceived status.

This is not to say that relationships between foreigners and Chinese do not happen. They still do, just on different terms. It is also important to highlight that for every Chinese woman who dates a Western man in order to better her own life, there are plenty more who date them from genuine affection. Many go on to marry their foreign boyfriends and create functional, happy families. A final point is that Chinese women trading romance or sex for wealth and security happens in exclusively Chinese circles too – it's not unique to foreign circles, as Gia herself is well aware.

I heard about a trend of high-school kids who are prostituting themselves. One story was of a girl whose first words on her nineteenth birthday were that she was so old. The story then went on to reveal that she had been a pimp for three years.

It was in Guangzhou. Also in the same province there is a factory town famous for prostitutes.

The town Gia refers to is Dongguan, a sprawling factory boomtown in the Pearl River Delta that boasts a population of approximately 7 million and a reputation as the Chinese capital of sex. Around 10 per cent of Dongguan's population is employed in the world's oldest profession. The sex workers – known locally as 'technicians' – are thought to ply their trade in thousands of side-street massage parlours, hotels, spas and karaoke bars. Dongguan has been subjected to various 'sweeping yellow' campaigns, as they are known; namely, official crackdowns on a trade which was outlawed in 1949 and yet continues largely unabated.

Poverty and desperation drive most to prostitution, but not all, as an advert from a 19-year-old girl looking to fund her travels around China through selling sex attests. Posting on her Weibo account in October 2014, teenager Ju Peng from Shanghai called for young, wealthy suitors to invite her to their hometown in exchange for a night of her company. Her critics have labelled her a prostitute; she retorts that she's more like a hitchhiker. Gia cites a similar example:

'A movie was made in Hong Kong that is typical. It is about a Hong Kong girl who goes into prostitution to afford designer handbags. The kids want money without really putting in the effort,' Gia tells me. Of course it's not just Hong Kong and Dongguan that are tarred with the brush of prostitution – it's a defining feature of modern China, a seedy underbelly which undercuts narratives of China as orderly and sexually conservative.

DON'T CALL ME A FEMINIST

Gia challenges gender conventions through the medium of fashion too. Fashion has taken off in a big way in China. The country is no longer defined by drab suits and instead the streets present youths wearing a colourful array of different styles. If anything, fashion is one of the areas in which young people are expressing their identities the most. While the country's young fashionistas are not quite as daring as the famous youth in Tokyo's Harajuku neighbourhood, they are becoming increasingly conscious of brands and appearance.

Gia is fully aware of this and is capitalising on it through her own T-shirt line. The simple black and white cotton vests feature anti-establishment slogans splashed across them and are sold at various boutiques in Shanghai and Beijing. Enthusiastic about this side project, she gets out her iPad. A few clicks later and we are wading through an array of other designs, which range from the sanitised (an image of an inward-looking eye, for instance) to the explicit ('Another pussy you can't fuck').

> It doesn't have to do with sex. It's more like an attitude towards sex. They're about love and devotion in relationships. The inward-looking eye represents miscommunication between couples; this T-shirt – with the shape of a vagina and the words 'eat me' in Chinese – are about how passion and communication are both important.

With the songs and the T-shirts, Gia represents the most confident, outspoken Chinese girl I know. And yet she is still reluctant to call herself a feminist. The word makes her feel uneasy. It's not from an intellectual perspective – some key Chinese scholars of gender have persuasively argued that the word is too Western-centric to describe the Chinese situation. Rather, Gia is concerned about the negative connotations of the word.

Whether feminism needs a change is a question that has been bothering feminists for some time in the West. Connotations of bra-burning aggressive women have stopped many women from identifying themselves with the movement in the past. In recent years, however, feminism has come back into the mainstream and more and more women are wearing the label with pride. The same is not the case in China. Even though Gia describes her music as riot grrrl, a movement closely aligned to other feminist subcultures, she doesn't describe herself as a feminist, joking that Chinese feminists cannot find boyfriends, and it is difficult enough finding a boyfriend in modern China. Chinese men don't like strong women, she adds, echoing common parlance about alpha females and beta males not finding spouses in a market where men marry down. She seizes my notepad and draws a scale of A to D, placing herself at the top, A, showing how lonely a place it is for the Chinese female.

'True gender equality is impossible in China. In my late teens and early twenties I still harboured hope. Now I don't think it's possible,' she tells me. She believes China lacks the social foundation for true female equality. 'All the problems in China are created by men. Chinese women are by nature the more passive sex. The route of inequality here is that women do not have their own choice, while men do. So if men don't want to marry them, then it's not their fault,' she says.

Consequently, for all her independence, Gia still stresses about finding a boyfriend, like some others here. She just isn't in as much of a rush. She doesn't see herself as a leftover woman, which she believes encapsulates white-collar workers and girls who really want to settle because they lack their own life goals (a slight misunderstanding of the term, perhaps). Her sympathies rest with these women; their fates are largely out of their control and the term is the creation of men. At the same time, she is still affected by gender norms. Her story shows just how deep these conventions run and, if anything, just how desperately China needs more women like Gia and, more to the point, women like Gia actually to call themselves feminists.

We sit in silence. A few moments later she jumps up from her couch and enthusiastically tells me that she is working on a new album, which should be released shortly. Quentin Tarantino is a huge influence in her life. Do I like him, she asks? She deeply regrets having turned down an invitation to a party he hosted while he was filming *Kill Bill* in Beijing, she quickly adds as she manically races through sentences. She has created a new song inspired by the movie, called 'Kiss Kiss, Bang Bang', and flicks her iPad back on, clicks 'play' on the song and puts the tablet into a simple cardboard shoebox, which acts as her speakers.

An electro beat hums out from the box, with a chain of indecipherable words layered on top. Gia starts to dance around her living room. I leave the interview with a sense that while some battles might be won in the world of Chinese feminism, the war still continues.

CHINA'S NOW GENERATION

10

Leaning In
Women and China's New Power

We are the golden girls.
29-year-old attendee at a singles event

It's an interesting moment to be a career woman in China, full of both hope and frustration. On the more positive side, there has been a lot of attention paid to the number of female millionaires in the country. According to the 2014 Hurun Global Rich list, 17 of the 358 US-dollar billionaires living in Greater China are women (up from 14 in 2013), and 19 per cent of Chinese women in management positions are CEOs. The perception that women are on the rise has even led to the coining of a phrase – *yin sheng, yang shuai* – which means the female (*yin*) is on the up, while the male (*yang*) is moving down.

Beneath these encouraging statistics, however, a different world operates, a world in which women are severely disadvantaged when it comes to the workplace. The ability of women to outperform men financially is very restricted. According to the All China Women's Federation, urban Chinese women in 2010 earned 0.67 yuan for every 1 yuan men earned. More depressing still, the gender pay gap is actually increasing. In 1990, urban Chinese women earned 0.78 yuan for every 1 yuan men earned.

Cutbacks are happening elsewhere. Chinese women hold a diminishing number of seats on corporate boards, according to the All China Federation of Trade Unions. In 2005, women occupied 43 per cent of board seats in China, while in 2011 the number was down to 32 per cent. Nor has it gone unnoticed that there are no women in the current Chinese Politburo, which was formed in 2013. Given that the Politburo is only renewed once a decade, China is not going to see a positive female icon in a position of power any time soon, which doesn't bode well for resolving gender inequality in the workplace. In fact, the last time a woman really entered the political fray was in the form of Gu Kailai, Bo Xilai's wife. Her portrayal in the media was that of Lady Macbeth, as she was sentenced to imprisonment for murder. It remains to be seen how far this sends out a negative message for any females who might dream of higher office.

The pressure to marry young and a prevailing belief that men are more committed to their work life is definitely playing a role in continued disparities. Other factors contribute too. One particularly strong cultural norm that directly affects Chinese women's ability to break the glass ceiling is the way business is conducted in the country. Going to KTV – Chinese karaoke bars – is a central part of conducting business. This deters women, as karaoke joints are synonymous with prostitution. The KTV hostesses are not just there to serve clients drinks, something which Zheng Tiantian outlines well in her book *Red Lights: The Lives of Sex Workers in Postsocialist China*. Karaoke has become the Chinese equivalent of men doing business at a strip club and yet goes a step further. Reportedly there have been instances of men having sex in front of co-workers. As Tiantian points out, sex has become a currency which men use to show off business bravado. Women are to a large degree excluded from these male-bonding pursuits, which has huge ramifications on their ability to move up the corporate ladder.

Even when business is conducted somewhere less risqué, it is still not as open to women. Banquets – another business staple – are liquor-laden affairs. Drinking is very much a man's sport, to the extent that my Chinese teacher told me that when she returns home, her brother can drink (and smoke) to his heart's content, but she is admonished by her mother, who says it is not ladylike, for doing so. The culture of banquets and of drinking means that women struggle both to form the right bonds and to gain access to the right opportunities.

BEAUTY CAPITAL

Women must also compete amongst themselves. In China, where applicants often attach a photograph to their CVs, some jobs require women to measure up to a certain level of attractiveness.

'The dramatic economic, cultural and political changes in China have produced immense anxiety experienced by women, which stimulates the belief that beauty is capital,' comments Wen Hua, author of *Buying Beauty: Cosmetic Surgery in China*.

The pressure to conform to a certain beauty ideal in order to secure a job has given rise to a spike in plastic surgery. According to the International Society of Aesthetic Plastic Surgery, China is the world's third-largest market for cosmetic surgery, after the US and Brazil, with more than 2 million operations annually. The number is on the rise, doubling every year, announced China's vice health minister Ma Xiaowei at a conference in 2011 organised by the national Health Ministry.

According to Wen, cosmetic surgery is most popular among women struggling to find employment. For example, certain government positions request women to be above a certain height, as they often do for men too, usually north of 1.58 metres. Some women have gone to desperate lengths to achieve this, forking out cash on dangerous, painful leg-lengthening procedures.

'The belief that better looks secure better jobs has pushed more and more Chinese college students to spend lavish amounts of money on cosmetic surgery,' Wen writes. Wen also says attitudes towards plastic surgery in China are much more accepting than attitudes in North America. Chinese parents can be critical of their children getting tattoos, claiming that they should not alter the body their parents gave them, and yet there are plenty of examples of parents paying for their children's surgery.

I speak to Wen about whether the situation has changed since her research back in 2006–7. While plastic surgery is still rife, there are fewer job ads asking for women to conform to certain fixed aesthetics these days. However, this is not a cause for celebration.

'Gender discrimination in employment still widely exists in China's workplace in different ways that are hidden. The discrimination has changed from overt to recessive, whilst the situation might be even worse because hidden prejudice and discrimination against women is harder to avoid and punish,' she tells me.

It's a bleak situation, one outlined in Leta Hong Fincher's *Leftover Women*, in which she debunks the popular myth that women have fared well as a result of post-socialist China's economic reforms and breakneck growth. The gains that women made under Chairman Mao have been dissolved in China's post-socialist era.

LEANING IN

As shocking as stories of leg-lengthening procedures are, much of the more mundane, everyday discrimination common in the Chinese workforce happens elsewhere too. The pay differential in the UK, for example, is also shamefully acute, standing at 19.9 per cent in the private sector at the end of 2013, which represented an increase year-on-year since 2008. The US has seen an increase from 15 per cent in 2004 to around 17.5 per cent in 2013. As headlines attest, the global recession has dealt a major blow to female equality.

The biggest difference between China and other countries lies in women's ability to challenge these practices. With a government that clamps down on civil society, Chinese women are often isolated. Few groups are campaigning for gender equality. But recently some have emerged. Beijing's Lean In movement is one such group.

Inspired by Facebook Chief Operating Officer Sheryl Sandberg's bestselling book *Lean In: Women, Work and the Will to Lead*, which has been translated into Chinese and sold copies in the hundreds of thousands, the women's professional development group was established in 2013. It was the first Lean In circle in China. Since then others have opened across the country, and top universities are holding 'Lean In' discussions.

The group organises a variety of social activities to discuss the information in Sandberg's book and to elaborate on how Chinese women can achieve their professional goals.

Lean In Beijing is just getting started when I approach the girls behind it. They have recently received a big psychological boost in the form of Sheryl Sandberg meeting them during a trip to China and are still gushing about it.

The first woman I speak to introduces herself as Rose, a teacher from Hubei Province, who says she has started her own classes – Learn English from American TV Series. She hopes to be an entrepreneur in the education field in the future. Rose says she is fortunate enough to have little experience of sexual discrimination (that she is aware of) and adds: 'I think 90 per cent of Chinese women lean out in 90 per cent of situations where they should lean in, since we are educated to be soft and not aggressive.' For her the appeal of Lean In Beijing is being part of a support network which extends beyond close friends and family, something she feels is distinctly lacking in China.

Next I talk with Chao, aka Clover, a 25-year-old HR coordinator who works in the telecommunication industry and is involved in Lean In on the side. Clover is more forthcoming than Rose and offers clear insight into the workings of Lean In in a Chinese context.

She was born in north-eastern China, 'a freezing cold place', as she describes it, and moved to Beijing two years ago after graduate school. I ask Clover how she first heard of Sandberg and her Lean In theory. After all, while Sandberg's book might have been published in Chinese, Facebook is still banned and therefore news relating to Facebook doesn't generate as much clout in China.

'Girls' self-growth and tech innovation are my major passions. I read tech news all the time,' she says. 'I got to know about Sheryl Sandberg's success in Facebook a long time ago. I watched Sheryl Sandberg's TED talk, "Why We Have Too Few Women Leaders", and I loved it. Then I read her book *Lean In* and I knew I needed to recommend it to all of my female peers.'

In some ways Clover has had a different experience from the one we might expect. She describes her company as doing well in terms of lessening sexual discrimination, although she admits that it still has far fewer women leaders than men. Her biggest concern is the attitude of her Chinese female counterparts.

> We blame men all the time for any discrimination women face. But I think I've faced more discrimination from my female co-workers than from their male peers. When I showed high working performance, I could easily gain respect and trust from my male teammates, but not so easily from girls – they are better at encouraging and complimenting men's success.

Women start off in the same place, wanting to do well at school (girls' grades outstrip boys') and wanting to get a decent job. Then said ambition trails off.

> To me I feel every girl and woman in China wants to fulfil some professional dream, at least once in their lifetime or especially when we are young. Girls are quite competitive in school and often perform quite well. But once we step out of school and enter society, all of the goals turn to the pressure of marrying a good husband. It becomes the major standard of how we evaluate our life. We deliberately make our lives all about men and relationships. For example, every time I have a girls' gathering, the topic is always about boys. It makes me quite disappointed.

Clover got involved in Lean In Beijing when she was approached by Mariel, one of the co-founders of the group. Ever since, she has been working hard to spread the Lean In concept and help more women in China find a circle they can join and gain support, experience and strength from.

Looking forward, I want to know what's in store for Lean In. How are the girls confronting such deeply ingrained gender stereotypes?

'From my understanding, courage is one thing that Chinese women are lacking when it comes to making major life decisions, asking for a job promotion, or even simply choosing to do something for themselves instead of for others,' Clover tells me.

When we are faced with these problems, there isn't a place or people in our lives to share our professional resources or to encourage us. The meaning of the Lean In circle is to create a private and comfortable environment for women to learn, to share and to support each other. If we want society to recognise us, we first need to recognise ourselves. Therefore we set the mission of Lean In Beijing to help women build or find their own circles.

She adds, when I ask her about her feelings concerning the future: 'I've witnessed the rapid change in people's awareness of gender equality in the past ten years and I think an era for women to have diverse life choices has come to China.'

I have reservations about the Lean In movement myself. As much as the manifesto has done a lot for a niche group of women operating at the top of the business world, it glosses over the hurdles the average woman experiences. In the case of China specifically, it's excellent that the country now has an established network of women opening up a conversation about women's roles in the workforce – it's a first, and better than nothing. However, I don't share Clover's positivity about the future. It's going to involve a top-down approach as much as a bottom-up one to level the playing field for women in the Chinese workforce and to help destroy the stereotype that China's women are material girls waiting for a rich husband to take care of them.

THE GOLDEN GIRLS CHALLENGING CHINA'S GREAT WALL OF DISCRIMINATION

At a Chinese matchmaking event I go to (which involves games and no alcohol, sort of like a children's tea party for adults) I meet a few attendees and question them about their reasons for coming. One girl particularly stands out. She has a big goofy smile and a short bouffant haircut. She has ended up at the event after being invited by a friend. Both the girls are here to meet other people on a social level as well as a romantic one. She is 29. It naturally invites the question; does she feel a lot of pressure to get married? She shrugs and laughs simultaneously. Being single at 29 is not a negative, she tells me; it is a reason for celebration.

'We are the golden girls! We can make our own paths in life,' she enthuses, her grin growing wider. 'We have independence. Life is good.' She still wants to get married, just not yet. The age of 35 seems about right, she calculates out loud.

This conversation is one of several refreshing ones I have had with Chinese girls over the years, who are unwilling to be bullied by a scaremongering media and pushy relatives. Speaking to a few other people at the event, it becomes clear that many of the girls are there for similar reasons – the matchmaking is secondary to the socialising. The event is full of a new kind of Chinese woman, who is well-educated, confident, gregarious and seizing all the new opportunities available to her. This woman shows a different side to China's future, a side in which women are more central and in control than their predecessors. I meet this kind of woman at matchmaking events, in the workforce and plenty of other walks of life. Another such woman to cross my path is Yuxia.

Yuxia is a typical Beijing girl in many ways, having been born, raised and educated in the city. She still lives with her parents in their one-storey courtyard home in the city's north-west. She's using her strong sense of place to her advantage.

The 27-year-old has a business background, having graduated in International Trade. She worked at GlaxoSmith-Kline for four years and then moved on to the advertising giant

Ogilvy. These were enjoyable years. At the same time, they were not what she dreamt about. Instead, her heart was always in the catering industry.

'I'm a foodie in every way,' she tells me over four plates piled high with traditional Beijing breakfast. It is 9 a.m. on a Sunday and we are sitting in a restaurant-cum-bakery a few minutes walk from the home she has lived in since the age of six. The venue is packed, and not just with older early-riser types, but with the full gamut of Beijing's social scene. A strong smell of sugar and oil fills the air and the counter presents an array of goodies that could single-handedly keep the cardiac ward of any hospital in business.

Yuxia sits at a perfect 90-degree angle throughout our meal and is wearing a deep-magenta silk top and black tailored trousers, making her appearance less Sunday casual and more Monday work interview. As she tucks into a dense soup of red bean paste and peanut butter, she lists all the different types of food that she enjoys: Italian, French, Japanese, Sichuanese – particularly Sichuanese. The list goes on and is revealing – as more options are available to the youth of China, their tastes are changing fast. They're no longer content with a simple diet of local Chinese food, and the country's cities are constantly evolving to capitalise on this increasingly daring palate.

Yuxia maintains a soft spot for the local. In her case it is *jianbing*, a thin fried egg pancake that is the breakfast of choice for many Beijingers (and many of the city's clubbers, who eat it in the early hours on the way home). For Yuxia, while the Beijing take on *jianbing* is good, Tianjin, a city close to Beijing, has perfected the pancake.

'I want to bring Tianjin's *jianbing* to Beijing,' she says, eyes growing wider with excitement. On one of the plates a Beijing *jianbing* sits half-eaten. 'It's good. It just isn't as good as those in Tianjin.'

Jianbing is typically eaten on the go. As dawn breaks across Beijing, the city's street corners become home to vendors making the dish. Eating it on a plate with cutlery as we are doing is very unusual, and Yuxia believes a welcome change.

Specifically, she wants to open a small café where people can enjoy the snack at a more leisurely pace. She has already secured a business partner, a girl two years her senior whom she knows from university, and is looking for a venue to rent and a chef.

Her excitement is reined in by just a little bit of apprehension. The positive of living with her parents is saving rent. The negative is that she suffers from their lack of support on a daily basis. Her mother expresses a form of indifference to her plans, which would be manageable were it not for her father, who is outright against them. He thinks she's being unnecessarily risky and can't understand why his one and only child would leave a good, solid job.

His reservations are understandable to an extent, vocalised the world over, where parents want the best, easiest life for their kids. For the parents of China, though, the desire to see their children in a stable profession is more pronounced due to their own experiences of want and hardship when growing up. Yuxia's father was a child when China's Great Famine took hold in the late 1950s and early 1960s, which led to the death of around 40 million people from starvation, and he still remembers it. He also started his working life when the concept of the 'iron rice bowl' still held sway. This idiom refers to the system of guaranteed lifetime employment in state enterprises. Under the early Communists, city dwellers were divided into work units, where their basic provisions were met. Compared to those in the countryside, who still had to fend for themselves to an extent, a city government job was considered very desirable.

With the opening of the private sector from the 1980s, the situation changed. Ambitious workers flocked to this sector in search of better pay and prospects, and saw civil service jobs as a career dead end, a graveyard of ambition offering little more than security. The move even had a special name – *xia hai* or 'returning to the ocean' of private business.

In recent years the tide has turned a bit. Applications to the civil service have begun to increase: 1.5 million people registered to take the 2013 entrance exams, an increase of nearly 15 per cent year-on-year. A common reason for young people to apply is that they believe private-sector jobs are now too pressurised. This is compounded by China starting to feel the bite of the global financial crisis. Stability once again offers appeal.

Yuxia has no such qualms. She shows that for all the young people who are opting for stability, there are others who are less inclined towards it, or at least less so than their parents. For these kids, how much does the generation gap affect their choices? There's no easy answer to this and it will be context dependent. In Yuxia's case, it's complicated.

'I will listen to a bit of advice from them, but the big decisions I decide by myself. I want to have my life, not their life. Their life is too flat, nothing happens,' she says, referencing the fact that they rarely leave the city and have never left the country. 'My parents are different from US parents. US parents will encourage you to do something yourself, but the Chinese parents will not.'

Hers is a common enough attitude, that US parents allow their kids to have free rein. Newspapers run cautionary tales of Westerners gone wild, and people's views are formed to some extent through that prism, alongside TV shows available online, which rarely reflect a typical existence. Nevertheless, even if the reality of life is different to the shows, the typical Chinese parent is still more cautious in comparison.

This wariness manifests itself in other ways too. For example, every time Yuxia's father enters her bedroom he lectures her on her spending habits. Yuxia likes to spend a decent chunk of her salary; her parents want her to save. Research from a few years back shows that the average household in China had four times more savings than that in the UK, but times are changing – the youth of China are more happy to open their wallets and pay for consumer goods and leisure activities.

Fortunately for Yuxia, her parents do not actively interfere and have, somewhat surprisingly, placed no pressure on her to get married. It's a relief as Yuxia is newly single. She tells me briefly about her ex. The two had met at a large Beijing club, which she says is quite an unusual setting to start a serious relationship.

'People's common thoughts are that the boy and girl who are in the clubs have their purpose [sex]. People will think the girl is slutty and the boy is a playboy. The normal way is to meet them in a restaurant or KTV [karaoke],' she tells me.

They went on to date for seven years, breaking up when it became apparent he wanted marriage less than she did. Since their split, instead of desperately trying to find a new boyfriend, Yuxia is happily concentrating on her own work plans and enjoying a break from men. As much as she still wants to wed, it is not her *raison d'être* at present. This is a new attitude in China – women are no longer tying their identity solely to that of wife and mother as they once did. The pressure to get married remains intense, but other identities are being forged and career ambitions are starting to feature in a more serious way.

'I want to be single for some time because I have been in a relationship since I was 16, so I haven't had any real single time for 11 years. I think single time makes you grow up. You can face yourself,' she tells me as she tucks her spoon into a final block of red bean paste. She then puts her cutlery down, defeated by the food.

Feeling jittery from all the sugar, we decide to head outside and go for a walk. Like many Chinese, Yuxia is enthusiastic about her hometown and keen to show it off to a foreigner. She takes me on a tour through the old lanes, a peaceful labyrinth of stone houses. The occasional willow tree obstructs the paths, which adds some green to the grey cobblestones. Finally we arrive at a red wooden door – the entrance to her home. Her mother has apparently invited me in, keen to meet the strange foreign girl asking her daughter all these questions.

'My mum really likes it when my friends visit. She will cook a lot of food and will drink *baijiu* [the famous Chinese spirit] with my friends,' she says.

We are about to step inside when Yuxia looks at her watch. Time has flown by and she suddenly realises she only has 30 minutes until her martial arts class starts, another one of her many projects of late. She walks me to the subway station – she insists. She also insisted on treating me to breakfast, much to my protestations. 'You are a foreign friend visiting my country. In China we treat our guests,' she keeps on repeating. I leave our meeting with the impression once again that China's only children aren't as selfish as the media makes out, nor are they as lazy. Months later Yuxia tells me that she has successfully set up her pancake café and with that I am also reminded that many young women in China are becoming more in control of their lives and destinies. They might not identify as feminists, but they are refusing to identity as leftover too, and the inclination towards collective harmony – which still exists – is having to compete with the surging force of individual interests.

11

Model Comrades
Youth, the Party and the Country

*Here everyone lies. We [actors] lie in front of the
camera, but they lie behind it.*
Sying, 28, an actor on Chinese TV

In the summer of 1962 a soldier at an army base in north-east China reversed his truck into a telephone pole, sending it crashing onto the head of a 21-year-old fellow soldier. The young man he killed was called Lei Feng. The Communist Party seized on Lei Feng as a model comrade: industrious, generous, modest and devoted to Mao. On 5 March 1963, in the lead-up to the first anniversary of his death, people were urged to 'Learn from Lei Feng' in a nationwide propaganda campaign. Mao's aim was to imbue China's youth with a passion for self-sacrifice and patriotism, and, historians argue, distract them from their own hardship.

Fifty years later, the legend of Lei Feng lives on, but it's not without complications in a country which has been changing beyond recognition. The propaganda campaign, which also includes the promotion of modern-day heroes and other model citizens, seeks to counteract a growing sense that China, preoccupied by seemingly ceaseless economic growth, is ethically unmoored. Some believe the young in particular need to learn from Lei Feng more than ever, concerned that they have lost their way and could benefit from a shining example. In the most drastic form of commemoration, Zhang Yidong, a charity worker from Anhui Province, announced plans at the start of 2014 to undergo plastic surgery to look like Lei Feng. He has already received micro-needle injections as part of his physical transformation.

Zhang's actions are at odds with others, particularly many young Chinese, who approach the legend of Lei Feng with a healthy dose of cynicism. An example of their cool disregard for the Communist icon occurred in 2013. Screenings of the film *Young Lei Feng* had to be cancelled in cities across China when no tickets were sold.

China's bloggers are also quick to highlight the double standard between a government that tells them to learn from Lei Feng and a government involved in a series of corruption scandals itself. Many now question whether Lei Feng even existed, or in the least achieved what the Party claims.

Whether Chinese youth admire or admonish the figure of Lei Feng, the fact remains that China is a country still deeply tied to its recent Communist past. Communist imagery is unavoidable, from the flags on buildings and soldiers on the streets to the paraphernalia on display in schools, universities and flea markets. Chinese youth are growing up against a backdrop of drab Communist colours as well as images of high fashion. And this is central to understanding the experience of young Chinese: as divided as the nation might be about how legitimate the Communist Party is, it's still incredibly important to people of all ages. When it displays messages of leftover women and the like, these messages are more often than not absorbed because the Party remains fundamental to modern Chinese life. Therefore, any examination of Chinese youth and their relationships must take into consideration the relationship between themselves and their governing body.

The Chinese Communist Party (CCP) is the largest political party in the world. According to the Party's own statistics from 2012, some 85 million people are members, representing around 7 per cent of the population. This number is increasing by an average of 1 million each year.

The composition of the Party is mixed. More than 44 per cent of new members are front-line workers, such as industrial employees, farmers and migrant staff. This leaves a gaping hole filled by university students and the moneyed population, who make up the bulk of recruitment. It's a huge contrast to the factory workers and peasants who constituted the Party's historical core.

Of the total Party members, 20.27 million are women and 5.80 million are from ethnic minority groups. Crucially, more than a quarter of members are 35 years old or younger.

There's no single motivation for why young people join the Party. Some join under pressure from their parents, for whom the Party loomed large during their childhoods. This generation continue to see the CCP as a safe refuge for their children against the economic uncertainties that continue to worry a developing nation.

Others join out of a sense of social responsibility and a belief in ideology. More appealing still, perhaps, is the fact that being a member of the Party is one of the best ways to get rich in a changing China. As a club, it provides connections, access to the best jobs and career stability. Membership in the Party is rarely stated in any job spec and open discrimination is forbidden under Chinese law. However, for those who want an interview after graduation, the facts on the ground are indisputable: Party membership is almost always a must for any form of government service and is strongly preferred for employment in China's vast state-owned enterprises (SOEs). Despite China's impressive market reforms, the 2012 statistical yearbook calculated that state enterprises employed 67.04 million people, which accounts for a whopping 30 per cent of all economic activity. A 2013 article in *Forbes* on the centrality of SOEs to the Chinese economy revealed that the country currently has around 20,000 SOEs, while the UK lists around a dozen.

The result is that China's non-Party employees are at a significant disadvantage. Certainly at the SOE I worked for, those with a mix of good *guanxi* (connections) and Party membership – the two being interrelated – rose faster than those who did not possess either, in what sometimes appeared like a game of snakes and ladders. For anyone wanting to work their way up the corporate world in China, Party membership is a huge advantage. For a secure and potentially hugely lucrative bureaucratic job, it's almost a necessity.

Thus the motivations behind joining the Party are mixed. That few are ideologically motivated seems to be of less concern for the CCP, which cares mostly about loyalty. In fact, the CCP itself contains a tremendous diversity of opinion, even at the highest levels, and reformists within the CCP apparatus arguably prefer that only some admitted to the Party are die-hard Communists. The anxiety caused by the deposed Party member Bo Xilai and his 'red politics' is evidence enough of the desire to keep radical policy out.

A career calculation is certainly what motivated Lili to join the Party. The 27-year-old applied for membership in her first year of college in 2005. She was driven by a desire to become a civil service employee, with Party membership being practically assumed. She has since changed her career goals and now works for state media instead. That's where I met her, forming a close partnership at my old company.

'In the past, to be a civil servant was the only way out for me because in it you can get a good salary and a stable job,' she tells me over dinner. The words feel dramatic and out of place. We are dining at a Sichuanese restaurant in one of the busiest retail districts in Beijing. The shopping area, which has outside elevators and enough lights to power a small European country, feels very space age, as does the restaurant we are in, which glows from a mix of neon and glitter. Lili matches the surroundings. She has a very fashion-forward haircut – a fringe that stops halfway down her forehead – and is wearing designer attire. She has sported this look ever since I first met her and I had assumed she therefore came from a fairly affluent background. I was wrong.

Lili is from Beijing, born and raised. She currently resides with her parents in an old lane courtyard, which has managed to avoid demolition. Over the decades her parents have upgraded certain parts of the house. They've installed a shower, to ensure that they do not have to use the communal ones, but it's pretty basic after this. A toilet remains beyond their finances. Lili continues to use the public one, or a bowl under her bed during the cold, dark winter months.

Like other Chinese youth, Lili calculated that the best way to better her situation was to go to college and then get a comfortable government job. She felt more confident of her decision upon observing her cousin, who had been working for an international corporation and was completely exhausted by it all.

'I heard the civil service was less tiring. I was told that if I wanted to be a civil service member that I must be a Communist Party member,' Lili articulates, adding, 'Also the chances of getting promoted are bigger within a state-owned enterprise if you are a member.'

Lili has a proclivity for straight talk. As she confirms how popular it was to become a member at college – eight out of ten students now want to join the Party, according to a recent survey by the Ministry of Education – she admits that part of the reason for applying was rooted in a desire for power, both on an egotistic and a pragmatic level. A government job – often referred to as an 'iron rice bowl' – has cachet and with that cachet come sycophants. Being a Party member comes with a list of perks well beyond just employability, as people cajole and bribe members to better their circumstances – just as some in Beijing use sex or a relationship to better their lives, others use the Party.

Sadly for Lili, membership wasn't quite the golden ticket in terms of employment. She passed the civil service exam only to fail at the interview stage. Reflecting back, she thinks it was because she did not have the right *guanxi* (connections), her suspicions rooted in the fact that her friend was accepted at the same time that she was rejected. The friend never even passed the entrance exam, but her uncle was a *chengguan* (local official) and from this she got a firm foot in the door.

Becoming a member of the CCP is a lengthy process. It took Lili four years, from 2005 to 2009, though in actuality the process started much earlier.

The foundations of the bond between a Chinese person and the CCP are usually laid in primary school. Most Chinese children aged 6 to 14 are members of the Young Pioneers of

China, which is under the auspices of the Communist Youth League. The kids are usually unaware of precisely what they have joined; they only know that they have to wear a *hong ling jin* (red scarf) once they become a Young Pioneer. Upon joining the Young Pioneers, they are also asked to vow: 'I love the Communist Party of China, the motherland, and the people; I will study well and keep myself fit, preparing to contribute my efforts to the cause of Communism.'

At the age of 14, Young Pioneer members automatically exit the organisation and are given the opportunity to join the Youth League, a more important organisation. One of the perks of this membership is that it makes it easier to become a Party member later down the line. The Youth League has served as a launch pad for the ascension of many of China's current top leaders, such as former president Hu Jintao. Its alumni list is impressive.

A lot is required of members and therefore for most Chinese, their personal affiliation with the CCP stops at Youth League level. For those who stick at it, rising within its ranks can be tough, especially if you're from an ordinary background – in other words, no political background. For these people, upward movement involves a mix of personal charm, capacity for work, strong *guanxi* and plain old good luck.

Lili managed to rise up the ranks of the two junior institutions and continued her upward trajectory at college. The first step for her – and others – was to apply to the Communist Party branch at her university by sending in a handwritten letter expressing her intent to join. This always takes a certain formula, namely an outline of exactly why the person wants to become a member, what they know about the Party and what they will do once they are a member. Lili's application was original, she reckoned, against the hordes of others who typically copy and paste from the internet.

'My grandfather was a Communist Party member, having enlisted during the Sino-Japanese War in the 1930s. He was quite well-respected in his compound,' Lili tells me.

My grandmother [still alive] is also a member. My grandfather would tell me stories of his time as a soldier, stories that proved perfect narrative for my application. He served in the infamous Eighth Route Army and sent an important message to the Balujun during the Japanese War of Aggression [as it is called on the mainland].

The story of her grandparents caught the attention of the recruiters at university, enabling her to get through to the test round of the application. This involved attending weekly classes in which she learnt all about the history of the Party and what a Party member should do; namely, leading people to push China forward and being a pioneer in life and work.

It felt like an opportune moment for me to ask Lili her thoughts on Mao, the Great Helmsman, as he is sometimes called.

'Mao was a person who had led people to crack down on Japanese invaders, the Kuomintang and landlords. He had liberated poor people, especially farmers and peasants. This is part of true history,' she declares almost as if she was reading from a book. He was a good person then, I ask?

I was told by my father that he was a really good person, but when I grew up I read bad things. My father was only seven when the Cultural Revolution started. He said that because we have no experience to borrow from, Mao just followed in other people's footsteps [non-Chinese] and was misled by the people around him. So now I think half–half, but the good part is larger than the bad, probably 60 per cent to 40 per cent.

At some stage the idea arose of weighing up Mao's character according to a percentage system. Lili's ratio is incidentally less flattering than the official line – that Mao was 70 per cent good and 30 per cent bad. Lili keeps her more jaded views of Mao quiet. She knows exactly how to play the game. At the end of every term, she was made to write a 'thought report', in which she outlined her progress and her opinions on society – all glowing of course.

On top of attending classes and writing reports, Lili had to act as a model comrade. She could not be seen to do anything that was 'ideologically incorrect'. This covered the normal stuff – drugs and other scandalous behaviour – alongside generally making sure that any critical views were kept to herself. Throughout this time she saw several of her competitors drop out.

After three years she was finally accepted. It was an anti-climax in her life, and in the dinner conversation. I expect to hear about an award ceremony or at least some kind of celebration. Instead she tells me nonchalantly that she was just called into an office at the end of the process with the remaining candidates and half were told they had made it, the other half not. There were no tears from the unsuccessful ones and not much enthusiasm from the rest. All of that and no civil service job at the end. It's a lot of effort.

It's still costing her too, both in terms of time and money. Lili has to attend regular local meetings and help select delegates to attend the national ones. She has to donate a small amount of her salary each month to the Party. Sometimes this fee goes towards outings either for fun or for charity. Mostly, though, Lili reckons it just goes into a deep hole.

Throughout our conversation Lili has been attacking a big bowl of fish which is drowning in a pool of chilli oil. At this stage she puts down her chopsticks and starts doing some calculations out loud on her hands. She shakes her head over and over.

'There's no way I have got back what I have put in! Ha!' she fumes. 'No, no way.'

Despite this, Lili has no intention of leaving the Party any time soon. In twenty-first-century China, it's still better to be in than out.

'I think it's [the Party] half good and half bad. Because China is only ruled by one party there is corruption, which no one can change because the Party is the law maker,' Lili says of the negative sides when I ask. As for the positives:

Because China is ruled by one party it means things happen efficiently. An I will say it, I will do it kind of attitude. If there are two people, one can say that they don't want to do it. When there is news predicting the future of the country, the general argument is that two parties will be a disaster because there are a lot of different views.

I take a step back from the conversation to appreciate the irony of the situation. I am chatting casually to a Communist Party member in an expensive restaurant over expensive fish about the pros and cons of China's leadership. When Mao famously declared that a revolution was not a dinner party, he obviously did not envision Communist China of the twenty-first century. We go back to our food.

ACTIONS SPEAK LOUDER THAN WORDS IN CHINA TODAY

The CCP remains at the forefront of life in China through various avenues. In order to maintain its popularity and position within the country, the Party is reliant on propaganda. It's a dual approach: censors work 24/7 to ensure negative messages are isolated. Complementing their work are the actual propagandists – the people who help market the Party. Television and cinema are two of their biggest mediums.

Chinese screens have become a lot more diverse than in the past, showing reality TV shows based on Western equivalents, alongside the occasional Western film or show, but they are still controlled by a central governing body and their schedule continues to feature shows that are little more than PR for the Party. In the same way that CCP membership opens doors for young people starting out in China, so too does landing a role in one of these shows, as Sying attests.

Sying never wanted to be an actor. He wanted to study foreign languages at university and see where the wind would take him. It had been his father's dream to act and his father never got to see the dream come true. This is because Sying's father came of age during the Cultural Revolution (1966–76) and therefore formed part of what has been termed China's lost generation.

The Cultural Revolution was Mao Zedong's political campaign aimed at rekindling revolutionary zeal. Youths were at the forefront of the endeavour. Those from wealthy or intellectual families in particular were forced to leave cities and live with farmers, sharing their hard lives and, it was hoped, gaining new insight into the Maoist revolution. Millions packed their bags and moved to remote parts of China during this time. There, they transformed from students to farmers. Many stayed for as long as eight years in the countryside and only started returning to cities after Mao passed away, when a curtain was closed on the period.

By this stage it was too late for many to return to their studies. The result was disastrous. Without decent degrees or even high-school education, they were seriously disadvantaged in the modern workplace. Some managed to return to their studies; most did not and for a sizable chunk this meant surviving on state handouts or whatever they could make from the underside of China's economy. In short, they were left behind in the race to modernise.

Michel Bonnin, a French sinologist and author of the book *The Lost Generation*, which explores the sent-down youth, talks of the difficulties they had in rehabilitating. *Zhiqing*, the name they go by in Chinese, have struggled greatly.

'Most people could only get labouring jobs when they returned,' he explained. 'And as they didn't have any specific skills considering the time they wasted away in the countryside, when it came to the 1990s, a vast number of *zhiqing* were laid off during the readjustment of many state-owned enterprises.'

Even those who remained in the towns and cities struggled. The Red Guards, the name given to Mao's student militia, took over their schools and universities, forcing academic achievement to be subservient to political indoctrination. Their hopes and dreams were shelved. Few won during this decade of turbulence. Hence the title 'lost generation'; a generation lost by the misfortune of their birth dates.

Sun Xiaoyun, Deputy Director of the Youth and Children Research Centre, commented in a report on the ramifications of the Cultural Revolution on the next generation of children: 'That special period of history ruined many parents' golden years. Their dreams were blown away. So they tend to place all their hopes on the next generation.'

As Sun highlights, these parents would often display unshakable determination to see their children live more enjoyable lives than they did, taking advantage of the many more opportunities available to them. Thus the *balinghou* – the children born in the 1980s – have suffered a triple burden: that of being only children; that of being born into a country which places the ambitions of parents as paramount; and that of being born to parents whose dreams were scuppered during the 1960s and 1970s and who want to live through their children more so than ever.

The story is no different for Sying and his family. His father was born in 1955, which made him 11 years old when the Cultural Revolution began. A few years into it, at the age of 15, he was forced to move to the north-east, to Heilongjiang Province, where he worked for the army.

The assignment was not wholly unexpected. At the time Sying's grandfather was in the military. He had been a general in the army fighting against both the Japanese during World War II and Chinese warlords. 'The warlords didn't kill him, but the medicine did,' Sying explains. He was allergic to penicillin and died one night in his sixties when given some. If his grandfather was still alive, Sying doubts he would have gone into acting – as has always been the custom in Chinese society, his grandfather was the most important member of the household through virtue of being old and male. Sying would probably be in the People's Liberation Army (PLA). Instead, he plays PLA soldiers on Chinese TV.

So Sying's father had pursued his father's – and the country's – dream and gone into the military. Sying pursued his father's dream and went into acting. For all the change, there's still symmetry.

While Sying's father was off driving tanks, Sying's aunt was faring far worse. She had been sent to the countryside, where she was made to rise early, feed pigs, then crop plants in knee-deep water full of leeches. It was brutal work. Damaged by the experience, she boarded a flight to Portland in the US immediately after the Cultural Revolution. Sying has never met his aunt and only knows of her story through his grandmother, one of the few members of the family who talks openly of this dark chapter of Chinese history. The aunt, meanwhile, is rumoured to be vocal about her adolescence, writing about it in the US in a genre known as scar literature (a term describing those people who have used literature as a way to come to terms with the experience. Jung Chang's *Wild Swans* is the most famous example).

Unlike his sister, Sying's father stayed in China. Not long after the end of the Cultural Revolution, at the age of 24 he met Sying's mother, who was also a soldier. She was three years his junior. The pair quickly married and Sying was born shortly after. They later moved down to Guilin, the southern city known for its natural beauty.

Sying had an idyllic childhood. He looks back on it as a time of playing in the great outdoors, with few worries and, very relevant to Chinese youth, clean air. He remained in Guilin until college, selecting a place at a niche drama school in central Beijing over attending a more mainstream one, which he tells me would have been his personal, first choice.

We have this exchange about his background over WeChat, a Chinese instant messaging service. Sying punctuates most sentences with emoticons, as is common amongst young Chinese, who can and do carry on entire conversations with them.

I had met Sying a year prior to this conversation at a club in Beijing. Initially it was romantic, but that was short-lived. Out of the ashes of our fling, a nice correspondence has arisen.

A few weeks on from this latest conversation we meet face to face. Sying shows up wearing khaki shorts and a very low-slung

V-neck T-shirt, so low in fact that I can almost make out his belly button. Drawing further attention to his exposed upper half is a cross, dangling from a thick black thread wrapped around his neck. It's his signature look, as if someone has told him that his cleavage is his selling point. The actor has a statuesque build, a symmetrical face, almost stoic in appearance, and a splattering of freckles across his nose. He is handsome by both Western and Chinese standards.

'I really need to make my body strong. An actor must be strong,' he tells me when I say he looks good.

Every day you get up early and sometimes you work from 6 a.m. until midnight or past midnight. So you need a strong body. Otherwise you will become very tired and ill. Also actors need to be able to run and shout, especially if in an action film. I was in a 1930s film set in Shanghai and I played the part of a spy. I was shot by a man and died in the arms of my lover.

It is statements like these that always endear me to Sying and it is no doubt his ability to deliver the most outlandish comments in the most deadpan way which make him ideal for Chinese TV, a medium that has garnered a reputation for fairly dubious acting.

CHINESE TELEVISION: TURN IT ON TO BE TURNED OFF

Although Sying is far from being famous, he is also far from being a nobody in the acting world. His face has appeared on shows on CCTV1 – one of the biggest channels – at 8 p.m., the primetime slot. His credentials are certainly enough to make his father proud; he regularly takes photos of the TV screen when Sying is on and shows them to his friends and colleagues.

Most of Sying's roles are under-challenging, he confesses. Quite often the characters on Chinese TV are very black and white. On top of acting that seems to straddle both wooden and exaggerated with little in between, the plots in the shows are fairly abysmal. My foray into the world of Chinese TV beyond reality shows has only lasted about 30 minutes, when I watched one of the most popular soaps. It started off with a slow-motion car crash and became more extreme from there. It was like *Casualty* and *Dynasty* combined, only with peculiar visual effects and more dramatic plot lines.

The shows also touch upon similar motifs. Given that the government tightly controls what does and does not appear on the airwaves, political messages are commonplace. The Sino-Japanese War, the fall of the Qing Dynasty – these are two topics which frequently appear on TV, all given the angle of the Communists being the creators and saviours of modern China.

I'm in good company not liking Chinese TV much. For the above reasons the Chinese themselves don't always tune into their own TV, save for talent or dating shows, which are notable exceptions. Many, particularly the young kids, favour Korean TV dramas instead, alongside US ones. When observers ask why China – the world's biggest nation – has yet to produce an international TV hit, they need look no further than these reasons. If the Communist government is going to continue to use TV to send its messages effectively, it might have to do so in a more nuanced manner going forward.

Of course, some shows are better than others, and Sying says he has been fortunate to land one he really enjoyed, even though the plot sounds alarmingly similar to those that people knock. It involved playing a Qing Dynasty soldier. The part, from his perspective at least, was quite complex and dynamic. The soldier unwillingly killed his beloved wife upon orders from the Emperor. He muses:

It wasn't stupid. Most of my roles are really stupid. Most producers are like 'Hey, Sying, you're really handsome, play this part.' But how can I act that? Being handsome is to do with what your character is like, not your face. It's how you act not how you look. I have bad memories of a lot of my roles.

On the face of it, Sying represents a success story of modern China. He is good-looking, popular and has a job that pays well. Except Sying isn't happy – like many of his generation, who are either exploited or out of work (unemployment among college graduates is approximately 10 per cent, while a recent survey revealed 53 per cent are dissatisfied with their jobs). These people are bitter and angry. Sying tells a succession of stories in which he has been taken advantage of, illustrating how ascent in the acting world, which is never easy, is especially difficult in China. The country's lack of trade unions and its business culture collide in cataclysmic ways.

'In Beijing the work is different from Hollywood. In China there are no rules about how to behave with employees. There is no actor's association [trade union]. We have no protection,' he explains.

The reality of acting is even worse for females in the industry. Their careers are cut short in a country that places a huge premium on young female beauty, and Sying says that, similar to Hollywood, stories constantly circulate about young girls being made to trade sexual favours for roles.

And, like in other professions in China, getting ahead in acting is much more about who you know than how well you can do the job. *Guanxi* – connections – are key.

Sying is also struggling when it comes to love, and again his story illustrates the contrast between the rhetoric and the reality of China's seemingly sociable and successful youth. Despite earning enough to afford a decent standard of living, he thinks it's not enough to establish the foundations for a successful family life. Specifically, while he has a car, he doesn't have enough to own an apartment and is doubtful he ever will if prices continue to rise as they have done in recent years.

'It [the car] is the most expensive thing I own. In Guilin people can pay for themselves, but in Beijing the prices are so high,' Sying says of not being able to get on the property ladder. 'Girls want stability, which I don't have, and right now I don't have enough money,' he adds.

Thus, for all of his fame, he still feels priced out of matrimony.

Sying's woes should be taken with a pinch of salt. It's true that he will struggle to raise a family on a less secure salary, but at this moment in time there's no reason he shouldn't be able to get a girlfriend, if he really wants one. As outlined throughout the book, while some women demand a level of income from a man, many do not. That Sying feels despondent in this respect is testament to how prolific – and unchallenged – these media messages are. Men are affected by gender stereotyping too.

Upon probing Sying further, one suspects the real reason he remains single is his pickiness. Sying has romantic visions of who Mrs Right should be: 'The right girl would be not lazy, she would work hard, be funny and definitely smart. Oh and beautiful – my parents wouldn't allow me to date an ugly girl. But I cannot ask for too much,' he tells me.

> I complain a lot that it's not fair. I was the best major in my high school but I'm not the best in Beijing. Most of the time I'm angry, angry with my work because no one tells the truth. That's the way people live in Beijing. Here everyone lies. We [actors] lie in front of the camera, but they lie behind it. I meet so many people that dirty my heart and I just try my best to keep it clean. I really miss my hometown. Now that I'm living in Beijing, I appreciate the life I had. It was good and healthy. I could breathe the air.

IDENTITY CRISIS

Sying's father's dreams are not Sying's. The catchphrase 'lost generation' has real resonance with Sying. In 2011 American photographer Adrian Fisk travelled around China photographing young people for his project iSpeak China. One particular encounter wedged itself in his memory – and mine. It was that of a young girl who went by the name Avril Lui in Guangxi Province. She held up a banner to the camera with a statement on it reading: 'We are the lost generation. I'm confused about the world.'

In an interview about his project, Fisk explained that the photograph struck a chord with many other young Chinese who viewed it.

'I think the pace of change has been so rapid in China in these last two decades that many of the young are in a spin which has left them somewhat confused,' he said. Their parents' generation had a clearer sense of what their identity was and what goals they were trying to achieve, even if they weren't always allowed to follow their own path. For the youth of today, these values have been turned upside down.

Fisk also believed that the message had a double meaning. The girl was directly referencing her parents' generation. Their inability to speak about or acknowledge the Cultural Revolution has had a direct impact on Chinese society today. 'There is a sense amongst some young Chinese that they have arrived; but, where from, and has it been worth it?' Fisk commented.

I have observed this too. Broadly speaking, young people in China are divorced from their country's recent history. They've no memory of Mao Zedong and glean little from a censored environment. Their grandparents still fill their conversations with references to key dates in the past. They (their grandparents) are very grounded by and locked into the country's history, but their parents are unlikely to talk of their own experiences, leaving them trying to second-guess the roots of twenty-first-century China. Their thoughts can be jumbled, which goes some way in explaining the popularity of time-travel literature and film amongst China's youth. These typically involve a character from the present day being transplanted back in time to some ancient dynasty. So popular is this medium that at one time the government tried to ban it, claiming that it was manipulating history. But with a government and population unable to talk honestly about its recent past, the youth are left to put the pieces of the puzzle together themselves.

For many youth, the time-travel genre has echoes in the present day. As Sying's longings to return to his childhood hometown attest, the present reality of life in Beijing is not easy. Chinese youth don't always want to occupy the here and now because, put simply, it isn't always that pleasant.

Sying certainly feels ambivalent about the present. 'There is so much corruption,' he tells me, shrugging. 'You can see from Beijing that the rich are becoming richer and the poor poorer, so where is the government?'

Sying's father fans the flames of his discontent. He has since left the army and joined the police force. There he encounters a lot of corruption, which he tells Sying about. Both men, though, separate their criticism of local government from criticism of the Communist Party at large, which for them – and many others – remains beyond reproach.

'As much as I don't like the government, China is very safe. There's not much crime. No one can use guns. The economy is very good.'

It is this ability to separate criticism of local government from the national level which helps the CCP stay in power and grow in size. The question most often asked by those with a fleeting interest in China since the country's 'rise' has been about the fate of the Party. Will it manage to maintain control as the country becomes wealthier and the internet becomes more important, or will it go the way of the Soviet Union? Without being a fortune-teller, no one can provide a precise response. And yet, looking at these anecdotes, the Party is not going anywhere for the time being.

A few months later I speak to Sying again. He is doing better on all fronts. He has landed a role in a Chinese TV show and has decided to join an acting group, in the hope that they will provide him with the support he otherwise lacks. Although he is still single, he is optimistic about the future.

'We used to have the American dream but now we have the China dream,' he tells me, looking ahead, as so many other young Chinese now do.

CHINA'S BIGGEST FANS:
THE RISE OF YOUNG NATIONALISTS

For all of Sying and Lili's personal misgivings about the Party, they steer clear of criticising the system as a whole. Theirs is a typical stance. Like many others – not just in China – they have enough on their minds without familiarising themselves with their country's politics. In lieu of a major shake-up, they look to the post-revolutionary landscapes of Russia and Syria as evidence of the undesirability of political change. Democracy, for now, is out of their reach and therefore divorced from their reality. Hence interest in the leadership change in 2012 was minimal amongst the young, whereas the youth of the US, by comparison, were fired up about their elections, which took place concurrently.

That said, Chinese youth can be politicised about the issues that directly affect them. In the rising number of protests across China, which often hinge on the ubiquitous complaints of poor working conditions, pollution and corruption, young people have played crucial roles. Throughout they've seized technology as their greatest weapon. The shocking photograph of 23-year-old Feng Jianmei next to her bloody, forcibly aborted 7-month-old baby is a case in point. Tens of thousands of outraged Weibo users circulated and commented on the image, showing that they are willing to stand up to authorities if it's of immediate consequence. In this case, the One Child Policy is.

They care deeply about certain issues. It's just that these concerns mostly encompass the world of individual freedoms over collective ones. Reform trumps revolution. Many people I have spoken to say they like the idea of democracy, but it stays as that: an idea over a reality. Those who are more committed to a radical shake-up tend to be in the Chinese diaspora, part of an aggrieved ethnic minority, or to have lived or studied abroad. The most revolutionary types, paradoxically, are the nationalistic youth – the *fenqing*, as they are known – the 'angry youth'.

As China has become wealthier and more powerful on the world stage, nationalism has grown too. It represents a departure from the past. From the onset of the Opium Wars in the mid-nineteenth century to the end of World War II, China experienced several humiliating defeats at the hands of foreigners that knocked the nation's confidence. Now it is a force to be reckoned with, as are its youth.

I witnessed the most extreme show of nationalism during a 2012 flare-up of relations between China and Japan over the Diaoyu/Senkaku islands. Thousands of people took to the streets to protest outside the Japanese Embassy; Japanese cars and restaurants were vandalised; and my entire office became bedecked with Chinese flags.

Going by the label of China's most nationalist citizen is Rao Jin. The late-twenties male is a celebrity both within and outside China. He gained his nationalist credentials upon creating a huge blogging media platform called April Media, which also invited comparisons between himself and Arianna Huffington. The content of this blog was, initially at least, to serve as a receptacle for 'good China' stories against the 'bad China' stories that circulate in the Western press. As nationalist sentiment becomes mainstream, Rao Jin is providing an online forum for people to articulate their views.

I join Rao Jin and his friend for afternoon tea. It is a Friday and everyone has the day off as part of the celebration of the Mid-Autumn Festival, one of the most important dates in the Chinese calendar, when a dense pastry called a moon cake is traditionally eaten. Most people have gone back to their native hometowns to celebrate. The result is a much more subdued Beijing, one where getting a cab is easy and the pollution is low. It is a great time to be in the city.

We meet at a café in the Olympic area, a stone's throw from the Bird's Nest. It is a fitting venue for our meeting. Rao Jin rose to prominence in 2008, when he launched his blog – then called Anti-CNN – on 18 March in the lead-up to the Olympics. It was after a series of free-Tibet riots around the world, with the one on 14 March during the torch relay of the Olympic Games being the catalyst for him. Some Chinese, both overseas and internal, were upset by the way the Western press was handling coverage, believing the reports were misleading. Not least, Rao Jin says, photos taken in Nepal and India were used, and palmed off as being from Tibet.

'I wanted to tell the people the facts. I posted evidence on the internet of this. When I saw these pictures, I came up with the idea of showing mistaken reports to the world,' he tells me of the origins of his media empire.

On 18 March he set up a simple page called www.anti-cnn. com. He gathered people from all over the world to write behind a slogan that stated: We are not against the Western media but against Western media bias. 'I think there are many problems in China, but I think the Western media should respect the truth, which they didn't,' he adds.

Rao believes Tibet belongs to China. 'The Chinese military are just maintaining peace in Tibet. Subtitles say it is military force. That is not the truth. "China invaded Tibet" is not an acceptable sentence as Tibet is part of China. It is like saying China invaded Beijing.' The view of Tibet as just a part of China is one held by many within the country. Rao even believes that some people who were shown as wanting a free Tibet were actually hired. That the Western media only covered the free-Tibet protesters, rather than the thousands of Chinese students out to celebrate the Olympics, reeks of Western media bias, Rao believes.

'A friend of mine was on the subway in London and the Western media were all talking about how cruel the Chinese were being to Tibet – that's not true. A child pointed at him and said, "You Chinese people, you are all killers."'

Rao says all of this in a matter-of-fact manner. He is a well-turned-out man in his late twenties, incredibly confident and charming. Interestingly, while he holds his country in high regard, such flattery does not always extend to the government. He gets irritated when people ask him if he is a Communist Party member – he is keen to state he is not.

He adds, managing to avoid revealing quite what he thinks about anything:

The Chinese media do have problems that they cannot reveal because of the Chinese government. But the Western media report on the dark side. I am fine with it if it's correct. There are some topics that are sensitive, like Bo Xilai, Tiananmen Square etc. Every country has its laws. The more transparency the better. But the media have some sensitive topics that cannot be touched. It's complicated. The government attitude is if your speech doesn't bring people together, then you are okay.

Rao is clever; he knows that in order for his company to stay afloat, he must avoid heavy criticism of the government.

Whether one agrees with Rao's thoughts or not, he has certainly struck a chord amongst many Chinese. April Media has grown from a one-man show into a 20-person team, with a further 200 people writing remotely. Some are overseas scholars; younger ones come from Tsinghua and other top Beijing universities. Like the *Huffington Post* model, it offers a platform for aspiring writers and thinkers, people who are not household names yet and want to get their writing out there. At the time of meeting Rao, April Media has 1 million registered members and every day about 100,000 people discuss issues on its forum.

'Sometimes the government will telephone the website administrator and ask to delete a post, saying it is against the law. I can understand that. If you post some terrorist things on Facebook they will be removed,' he explains.

His bloggers write on all kinds of topics to do with current affairs, economics, social issues and the like. Rao describes these posts as 'constructive'. 'I appreciate those people who do not just criticise,' he adds as he pours me some tea with floating goji berries and pear chunks in it – a healthy choice, I am told.

Rao is in no doubt – China should play a more central role on the world stage.

It's really positive that China is more important. China's history shows China does not pick a fight. We won't invade others. It's good, peaceful and harmonious. Good for the rest of the world. China has one-fifth of the world's population so our own people will benefit. If one-fifth benefits, so does the whole world.

Despite personal misgivings about some of his views, it's refreshing to hear a counter-narrative to the one that says the younger generation are all self-centred little emperors and material girls.

Before April 2008, most Chinese government officials and scholars all thought the 1980s generation just watched US dramas etc. They were very Westernised. People thought they were very selfish. However, when they saw how they protected the torch in 2008 it made them rethink. They realised that they do care about the country, just in a different way to earlier generations.

Rao continues, 'My favourite city is Beijing. Beijing is Boston, DC, New York and LA put together. It has economics, politics, finance and history. Some people think Shanghai is the finance centre but the headquarters of banks are here, as are the best universities and talent. Beijing is plus, plus, plus!' It is one of the first times I have heard someone wax lyrical about Beijing.

As he says this, his smartphone comes out to show me photos of his favourite areas of the city. The Olympic Park, where he jogs, and the view from his apartment over the area. His positivity is boundless. I try to weigh in, to come up with counter-arguments, such as whether everyone is too focused on getting rich, but he always has a reply.

Everyone is benefiting from the economic boom of China. Each man in each country has a desire to get rich. It's natural. It's provoked by the gap between rich and poor. In Western countries you have fewer people and more resources. In China it is the reverse, so if you want to live better you've got to struggle your way to the top.

Rao has brought a friend to the tea, who shares a similar enthusiasm for China and Beijing. I ask her, when has she felt most proud to be Chinese?

'For me it's when I went shopping in the West and they said that they will accept Union Pay. Then I realised something really did change!' she answers in reference to the Chinese equivalent of Visa, which is now being accepted at more and more shops abroad. Her confidence in her country might still be pegged to Western acceptance, but the fact remains that her pride and willingness to defend her country is growing by the day.

As our pot of tea empties, Rao tells me he is single and hopeful about meeting a nice girl. He's in no rush to marry. He's only in his late twenties and as a male in China, the pressure has not been piled on yet. Instead, he's enjoying his life and all of the new options which are available to the youth of his country.

12

In Love with God
China's New Young Christians

I think God is saving the country.
Daiyu, 33

As we've seen, the youth of China are still prey to the forces of tradition, which have their origins in an amalgamation of different schools of thought, in particular Confucianism. These forces dictate certain rules, specifically filial piety and placing family at the centre of society. From these values it has been extrapolated that men and women must conduct themselves in various ways, such as marrying by a certain age and not having too many sexual partners before they do so. These are societal values; they are not religious ones, though they have been influenced by religion, and it's important to note that China is no stranger to spirituality and faith. It remains a deeply superstitious country, with a huge amount of rituals to ward off evil spirits practised by old and young alike. On the more structured end of the spectrum, there are also many practising Buddhists and Muslims. These two groups have been part of the nation's fabric for centuries. And now there's a newcomer: Christianity. It's having a huge impact on the personal lives of Chinese youth in particular, and if it continues to grow at its current pace, it has the potential to change the face of China, much as it has done in other Asian countries that have succumbed to it.

Christianity is enjoying a boom in China. Many people at the Chinese newspaper I worked for are practising Christians, and their numbers are swelling, especially amongst young people. Conservative estimates suggest there are 60 million

Christians in China. More likely it is over 100 million, as many are members of unregistered churches. That's a staggering amount, especially when placed in context: the religion has a chequered past in the country. The first records of Christianity in China date back to the beginning of the Tang Dynasty (618–907). Then, after two more notable fluctuations of success and failure in the thirteenth and seventeenth to eighteenth centuries alike, Christianity made another attempt of conversion from the beginning of the nineteenth century, as Western incursions in China had an impact on China's spiritual landscape.

It was not a big enough impact. The twentieth century dealt a series of large, almost devastating blows to Christianity. The May Fourth Movement of 1919 saw massive protests against the West and movements closely aligned to it. Meanwhile, the Communists deemed religion an enemy, or as Mao described it, 'poison'. From 1949 it was actively discouraged, albeit permitted in state-sanctioned churches, so long as worshippers gave their primary allegiance to the Communist Party. Later, during the Cultural Revolution, the eradication of religious life became a top priority. Christian activities, if not completely annihilated, were reduced to a minimum and went underground.

Deep beneath the surface, a different picture emerged. Rather than obliterating Christianity altogether, the adoption of such a hard line was arguably to Christianity's benefit. As the adage goes, what doesn't kill something makes it stronger. Chinese Christianity survived and, with a host of new Chinese martyrs created during the tumultuous years, it grew in popularity. Repression became a motivation for conversion.

After the death of Mao in 1976 the government continued to preach that religion was an evil, a line that continues today. However, since the 1980s, when religious belief was again permitted, official churches have gradually been able to create more space for themselves. This does not mean Christians lead harassment-free lives. Like Muslims and Buddhists, Christians practise their religion in the face of great opposition. Daiyu, 33, vouches for this. I meet her, a practising Christian, the day before I return to the UK. She has long wavy black hair and is wearing nondescript jeans, top and glasses. She explains to me that disparagement from other people in China has been one of her biggest obstacles to faith.

'Some people will say they don't know this religion and will think we are crazy. I met a guy several years ago and after he knew about my religion, he said I was a very good girl except that I believed in God,' she tells me, sighing in a way that conveys acceptance.

Much of the blame for this attitude can be laid on the education system, which engineers a degree of disrespect for religion. Daiyu was never taught religious studies at school, describing the purpose of her schooling as being very science focused.

'In our classes at school we were taught that religion is about people who are not educated enough. I was not upset by this, I feel quite blasé.'

During university, Daiyu was able to minor in religion. There she learnt about Christianity, Islam and Buddhism, but still from a Communist Party perspective. 'The teacher told us that after the course we would not believe in God. The teacher was a non-believer.'

Twenty-first-century China is no haven for Christianity. Nevertheless, it is a far cry from what it has been. That I am even meeting Daiyu is indicative. Finding a practising Christian in Beijing is easy, even without attending one of the many Sunday services that are notoriously busy. And many are willing to talk about their faith, under the veil of anonymity.

I meet her at a coffee shop on the ground floor of her office block. The office is located on Beijing's Third Ring Road. Throughout our drink, the faint hum of cars fills the background.

Talking to Daiyu about her religion is a bit like talking to an American as a Brit. The language is the same and yet the way it is used is different. Christianity in China differs from the way we practise it in the UK. For believers, it is definitely Christianity with Chinese characteristics. For example, Catholicism and Protestantism are categorised by the state as two separate religions rather than denominations, and they both report to the State Administration for Religious Affairs. In her Christian reading group, half study the English Bible and half the Chinese, and both have slightly different interpretations of the meaning, according to the translations.

And unlike in the West where proselytising is a firm feature of some branches of Christianity, it is strictly forbidden in China. Daiyu therefore does not convert people, aware of how sensitive the government is. The furthest she will go is to invite friends and colleagues to her church if they express curiosity. A Mormon friend testifies that it's the same story within the Mormon community; in exchange for being able to practise their faith, they must keep their heads down, or suffer consequences.

'Do you know of anyone who does convert people?' I ask, curious.

'Yes, I do know some people who try to convert people on the street. Equally I hear of people who have gotten in trouble for just that. Recently a South Korean church [in China] came into problems with the government.'

In order to isolate Christianity, any form of religious activity has to take place within a designated place of worship, not outside it. Most significantly, Chinese Christians sign up to the slogan, 'Love the country – love your religion,' an oxymoron if ever there is one since their country commits to the promotion of atheism at state level. In return for the believers' loyalty the government undertakes 'to protect and respect religion until such time as religion itself will disappear'.

The Christian landscape is divided into official and unofficial churches. The officially sanctioned Catholic Patriotic Association appoints its own bishops and is prohibited from working with the Vatican, although its followers are allowed to recognise the spiritual authority of the Pope. A larger Catholic underground church operates, which is supported by the Vatican.

The government is becoming more accommodating of the churches, ironically in part because of their commitment to the creation of a 'harmonious society', which they believe chimes with Christian values. For example, official interest in the Western evangelical Alpha Marriage Course has been expressed in light of alarm about the surging divorce rates. Christianity is seen as a good way to control the changing lifestyles of young people.

It's a self-perpetuating cycle: a more relaxed government policy regarding religion in turn spurs on the growth of religion. As China rises, more foreign pastors are coming to the country, and conversely more Chinese are travelling overseas, coming into contact with more Christians.

That said, the growing numbers do concern officials, not least since some Christian organisations align themselves with human rights groups. Under Xi Jinping's leadership there have been a series of crackdowns on Christians, leading to as much pessimism as optimism for the future of Christianity in China.

The reasons for people turning to the Church are often unpalatable to the authorities as well. China is said to be in the throes of a 'spiritual crisis' by both old and young. The old have seen their world turned upside down, as Marxism–Leninism has been transmuted into capitalism. For the young, trust is breaking down. Thus new converts span class and age lines, with peasants in the remote rural villages being just as attracted to the religion as sophisticated young, middle-class city dwellers, all driven to it by a sense that capitalism is rotting China's core.

'I think God is saving the country. People now are very shallow, they are not looking deep. The only purpose for them is money. For the Chinese, they think only the property they have will protect them. [They] don't have the correct attitude. I feel pity for them. Especially for the young people,' says Daiyu of her motivations for keeping the faith.

Daiyu is not a recent convert, having been a Christian from a young age. Her grandmother was the ringleader, who found faith straight after China opened up at the end of the 1970s, and she spread her religion to the girls in Daiyu's family (her father has never converted). Her faith has fluctuated over the years and is now as high as it has ever been, permeating her life in many ways. She has started studying the Bible every day for one hour at a time.

'Because I believed in God from a very young age, his influence is not felt suddenly but day to day. I can feel peace every day. China is not a very peaceful place. If you believe in God it helps. It relieves life pressures.'

Daiyu is particularly wound up by 'cheating' in China. 'For example, if an old person falls down, no one will help them for fear of repercussions,' she tells me. Daiyu is referencing a phenomenon plaguing the country. There have been examples in the press of people being in difficult situations in public without receiving help from passers by, such as Yue Yue, a 2-year-old child who was run over several times before someone stopped to help, by which stage it was too late. Most Chinese people attribute this to fear of being sued if they get involved, citing a 2006 case of a man from Nanjing – a former capital city of China – named Peng Yu who helped an elderly woman when she was hit by a bus. She then ordered him to pay a large portion of her medical bills. Almost every time a group of bystanders ignores someone in need (and these stories circulate often in a country of 1.4 billion), it becomes breaking news in China. Peng's story rears its ugly head. What is rarely mentioned is that Peng was forced to pay the woman's medical bills because police believe he pushed her in the first place.

If it is not a fear of lawsuits, what is creating this so-called bystander problem? Some speculate on other causes for why Chinese people are reluctant to get involved, such as China being a place where people compete for resources. The country has undergone intervals of famine and political turmoil for centuries, most recently during the Great Leap Forward, which saw tens of millions of Chinese starve to death in the late 1950s and early 1960s, and the ensuing Cultural Revolution, from 1966 to 1976, which turned family members against one another. These have affected the nation's social fabric. The idea that fellow citizens are people with whom you compete for survival, rather than people who can be counted on, is buttressed by reports from social scientists, who have discovered that people are less altruistic when basic resources are scarce or when they see survival as more competitive.

Other explanations have been offered. People are deeply concerned about it; it's a preoccupation for Chinese youth as they try to decipher their identity and place. For Daiyu, though, the cause is less important than the symptom. China is in crisis, and this spurs her to go to church.

Daiyu was raised in Hebei Province and attended services weekly as a child. She's from a small city, just big enough to house its own official church. Her recollections of early church attendance were of an older scene, and few members.

'When I was very young, I only knew old Christians. Now [in Beijing] we have young people. They come from all different classes. I was told many officials are there too,' she explains of her private church.

Although life in the country is not particularly conducive to being Christian, those who do practise usually do so with gusto. Daiyu, for example, is excitedly planning a visit with her church to Israel the following year, which will mark the first time she has left the country.

Christianity has become a comfort for Daiyu in many ways. She is 33 years old, still single and not that hopeful of finding a partner. Her beliefs help her deal with that fact and with the constant noise she is surrounded by from pushy relatives.

'Most of my friends feel lonely, even when they have boyfriends. When I am sad I feel the comfort of God. God leads me,' she states, without a hint of doubt in her voice.

Daiyu says she wants to get married, a U-turn from her younger self, who was more cynical. She tells me how in recent years she has felt weighed down by high divorce rates and her observation of many unhappy marriages. Daiyu is not alone in feeling this way. Outside Christian circles, there are those who are saying no to marriage entirely. Women in particular are absorbing stories of unhappy marriages and concluding it is not for them. Adultery followed by domestic abuse are the two most oft-cited causes for divorce in China. That women have few rights within a marriage when it comes to property, which is the biggest asset in China, isn't helping. They're getting the raw end of the deal in the event of divorce. Those who are engaged with this reality are choosing to avoid such a fate.

Daiyu, however, has changed her attitude after a recent encounter. A friend from her church told Daiyu that she has been happily married for 20 years and has never considered getting divorced.

'It's incredible to me. So now I have more faith in marriage.'

Daiyu ideally wants to marry a Christian. Judging by their numbers, her chances are good, and public churches organise matchmaking events too. Daiyu will also look beyond her church, as she accepts that even if Christians are growing in number, they are still a minority.

'In my church many wives are Christian first and then convert their husbands, so this is an option,' she says, a cunning smile taking over.

Asking a Chinese person about the ins and outs of their bedroom activity is embarrassing enough; asking a Chinese Christian is even more so. I take a deep breath and broach the topic of chastity.

'From the Bible I know you should not have sex before marriage. I think you should obey the Lord,' she responds, giving little away.

> I thought before that it was better to have sex before marriage as I would know if we were a good match. However, now I have changed my mind. There are too many divorces. If you choose one, you'd better not get divorced. Everyone has their own problems. If you break up with one then another one will have other problems.

Again she isn't really giving me a straight answer. She continues,

> I was on a dating site. I registered in 2008 and wrote that I was a Christian on it. I had no luck. So I stopped dating in

2010. After I dated several guys, I gave it up because I could not find my Mr Right. Later I realised it was my problem not theirs. I wanted to find a perfect guy and realised I was not a perfect girl. I need to be more accepting. However, I don't feel lonely. I never feel lonely. Most of the reason is because of God.

On some levels Daiyu must be the envy of her friends – she has found a way to block out a lot of the noise of modern China.

As the traffic on the ring road calms, Daiyu tells me it's about time she headed home. We say our goodbyes and I watch as she walks off towards the subway. It's my last night in Beijing for a while and I'm off to a restaurant that specialises in Beijing dumplings. Some 200 varieties are on its expansive menu, including my favourite, which are shaped like purple moons. I hail a cab and one pulls up instantly. I jump into the back and tell the driver where I want to go. He nods to show he knows and has understood. Then he looks at me in the rearview mirror.

'Do you live in Beijing? Are you here studying?' he growls in a husky Beijing accent. These are the two most oft-cited questions young foreigners get when cabbing in the city and I return my pre-prepared answer. A few more glances later, he asks my age. I tell him. Next, another predictable pry.

'Are you married?'

I answer that I am not.

'No?! You're not?! But you're almost 30! *Aiya*. Do you have a boyfriend at least?'

I shake my head again.

A look of disbelief overtakes his face. It's my last conversation in Beijing.

Epilogue
London

A couple of months after returning from Beijing, I am sitting at my desk in London typing away when a message pops up in my Facebook inbox. It is from a girl named Michelle, whom I have never met. She quickly tells me that she has read an article I have recently written about something unrelated to China and had been taken aback by my byline, which outlines the content of this book. She adds that she is Chinese herself, new to London and also writing a book about the country, which touches on similar topics. It is sort of *Eat, Pray, Love* in theme, only without the divorce part, as she describes it, and done from her own perspective. Bound by this common interest, she felt obliged to get in touch.

Several days later I find myself bonding with Michelle in person over experiences with men and with China. As we tuck into a dense slice of coffee cake in a café housed within a Victorian building, Beijing feels so close and yet so far away.

Michelle tells me that she is 28 years old and originally from Tianjin, the city near Beijing which is home to the famous breakfast pancake. Her parents left China when she was 12 and she has spent the better part of her teens and twenties in Canada, with occasional trips back to her home country to visit relatives still living there. In part inspired by China's rise and in part inspired by her own background, her mid-twenties saw her embark on two voyages across the country. She wanted to expand her experiences of it. More importantly, she wanted to find a Chinese boyfriend.

'I went back to China in search of love! At the time I really wanted a Chinese boyfriend. They treat you so well and it would make sense, you know, being Chinese,' she tells me as if this is a completely normal endeavour.

Michelle proceeds to dictate a list of amusing anecdotes in her quest for love. As she travelled, she seized opportunities to meet a wide variety of men. Some of them turned out to be complete weirdos – her words – and others nice, just not quite right. The climax was when her aunt enrolled her in the dating show *If You Are the One*, the programme in which the Chinese girl declared that she would rather cry in the back of the BMW.

The basic concept goes as follows: 24 girls stand in a line, each behind a lit counter. A man comes on stage, having already secretly chosen which girl he is interested in from a cursory glance at their bios and images. He announces some basic information about himself (name, age and origin) and at this point the girls can declare a lack of interest simply by turning off their light. If all 24 lights go off he loses and must go home alone; if not, he is in luck.

It is a winning formula, for Chinese TV at least. Shortly after it was launched in 2010 it was attracting around 50 million viewers per show. These figures rose after the infamous BMW episode. They then dropped off a bit; in response to public outcry over the quote the State Administration of Radio, Film and Television issued a set of new rules declaring that 'Incorrect social and love values such as money worship should not be presented in the shows.' Mention of salary and material possessions were banned, much to the disappointment of viewers, who found it less entertaining as a result. Still, it remains a key fixture in China to this day, particularly for the younger generation.

While the show is popular, Michelle was not. She kept her light on the entire time and yet never made it to the final three. She left alone, both from the show and from China itself. Her quest for the perfect Chinese boyfriend never reached its goal, though she tells me the project is ongoing.

It later transpires that I know other people who have participated in *If You Are the One*. Like Michelle, my friend Jerry was born in China and had a peripatetic upbringing, living between there and the US. Unlike Michelle, he was not looking for love from the show. As a man on it, Jerry's role was much more hands-on. All Michelle really had to do was turn up, listen and pass a fleeting judgement. Jerry's role was about performance. He could dazzle and, with millions of people watching, that was exactly his intention. No beating around the bush – he wanted to use the show as a platform to promote his new burger restaurant in Beijing.

Jerry knew of a few people who had been on the show, and so he applied, was interviewed and finally selected. Two field producers came to Beijing to tape him, which took the better part of a day, and weeks later he was once again in front of the camera before the whole nation. When on the show itself, Jerry decided to make burgers backstage for the three judges and to serve them on stage. Needless to say, Jerry was also not the most popular contestant. Despite being a native Chinese male in his mid-twenties and ticking most other key boxes – good-looking, tall, wealthy and Ivy League-educated – the female contestants sensed that he was insincere, a big red cross in the love market. He was voted off.

Both Michelle and Jerry's stories are fitting finales within the wider context of sex and youth in modern China. The two could not have approached the show any more differently, and yet they both failed. And this reveals an important truth: there is no single cut-and-dried rule by which youth are living and loving. For Jerry love is commodified, an enabler to get him ahead in the business world, as it is for the girls who marry simply for money, and for the businessmen who frequent karaoke bars to establish connections in the presence of hostesses. Michelle's reason for going on the show was fuelled by a genuine romantic urge, a quest for a Chinese Romeo which millions of other women – and men – are embarking on too.

It has been eight years since I first arrived in China, back at the end of the summer of 2006, bright eyed, bushy tailed and unaware of my own love affair with the country that was about to unfold. In those eight years China has aged a lot more than I have. We're talking dog years, not human ones. It is no longer the country of the future; it is the country of now. Mandarin is no longer something that the quirky Western kid learns at college; plenty of children study it as early as primary school. With that growing confidence, Chinese people aren't desperate to leave, to marry foreigners and establish better lives further afield in the way the cliché once ran. Instead, overseas Chinese return, expats forge permanent lives for themselves over there and most Chinese look to their own country for answers. Beijing smog is a problem and is driving lots of people, myself included, away from the city. Yet it is not quite the hardship destination that it once was. Rather, in my eyes at least, it is *the* destination.

China has an encyclopaedia-worth of problems and many people lead very difficult lives there. It is a country of intense poverty, of forced abortions and political imprisonment. It is still a country where to be above a certain age and single can be a death sentence to your love life and dreams of having a family. And it is now a country where that reality is hitting home for more people as the effects of 30 years of fertility policy are bearing fruit. It remains a country where the youth feel intense pressure: to work hard, to carry on family lines, to be the apples of their parents' eyes. What are headlines for us in the West are lived realities for those in China. In the week leading up to the submission of the first manuscript of this book alone, I received a message from a young girl briefly mentioned in the introduction, the one at boarding school in Chengdu. Since her reaching out to me about *Tiny Times* we have become pen pals of sorts and she messages me often. Then there was a hiatus. She apologised for this and told me a friend of hers had recently jumped to her death, the pressure of the college entrance exam apparently too much. Her message conveyed a tone of anguish rather than of surprise.

Some challenges have of course disappeared over the years and no doubt others will vanish in the future. Since I first started this book, for example, legislation has changed on the One Child Policy to allow couples where only one parent is an only child to have two children themselves. If this affects enough people, the implications are far-reaching for the social and economic fabric of China.

At the same time, other policies and attitudes remain stubbornly fixed or have mutated in ways that aren't necessarily improvements. Those who are upset about the nation's tapestry – the cries mentioned at various sections throughout this book – cannot be easily dismissed. Nor should they, and it will largely be up to the youth to decide the shape of things to come. As Chairman Mao said, they are the future.

If you had asked me back in 2006 whether the country would have moved in this direction, I would have had no clue. Similarly, I don't know what direction the nation is heading in now, what the youth will choose for their future. But I can say with certainty that it will be exciting, that it will surprise and that it will not fit easily into generalisations. With their many contradictions, China's little emperors and material girls have shaken up the nation and will continue to do so as the country boldly marches on in the twenty-first century.

Further Reading

BOOKS

Brownell, Susan, and Jeff Wasserstrom (eds), *Chinese Femininities/Chinese Masculinities: A Reader* (Oakland, 2002)

Burger, Richard, *Behind the Red Door: Sex in China* (Hong Kong, 2012)

Campbell, Jonathan, *Red Rock: The Long, Strange March of Chinese Rock & Roll* (Hong Kong, 2011)

Chang, Jung, *Wild Swans: Three Daughters of China* (London, 1991)

Chang, Leslie T., *Factory Girls: From Village to City in a Changing China* (New York, 2008)

Chu, Ben, *Chinese Whispers: Why Everything You've Heard about China is Wrong* (London, 2013)

Clark, Paul, *Youth Culture in China: From Red Guards To Netizens* (New York, 2012)

Gifford, Rob, *China Road: A Journey into the Future of a Rising Power* (London, 2007)

Guo, Xiaolu, *A Concise Chinese–English Dictionary for Lovers* (London, 2007)

Fenby, Jonathan, *Tiger Head, Snake Tails: China Today, How it Got There and Why it Has to Change* (London, 2007)

Fincher, Leta Hong, *Leftover Women: The Resurgence of Gender Inequality in China* (London, 2014)

Jacques, Martin, *When China Rules The World: The End of the Western World and the Birth of a New Global Order* (London, 2012)

Miller, Tom, *China's Urban Billion: The Story Behind the Biggest Migration in Human History* (London, 2012)

Min, Anchee, *Red Azalea* (New York, 2006)

Spence, Jonathan, *The Search for Modern China* (London, 1990)

Tiantian Zheng, *Red Lights: The Lives of Sex Workers in Postsocialist China* (Minneapolis, 2009)

Wen Hua, *Buying Beauty: Cosmetic Surgery in China* (Hong Kong, 2013)

Xue Xinran, *The Good Women of China: Hidden Voices* (London, 2003)

Yu Hua, *China in Ten Words* (London, 2012)

WEBSITES

(All URLs last accessed 2 February 2015.)

Ash, Alec, 'Chinese youth: do they dare to care about politics?', *Dissent*, http://www.dissentmagazine.org/article/chinas-youth-do-they-dare-to-care-about-politics

'The generation gap', *The Economist*, http://www.economist.com/blogs/analects/2013/07/generation-gap

Jaffe, Gabrielle, 'Performing *The Vagina Monologues* in China', *The Atlantic*, http://www.theatlantic.com/china/archive/2013/11/performing-em-the-vagina-monologues-em-in-china/281924/

Larson, Christina, 'Those big fat Chinese weddings', *Bloomberg*, http://www.bloomberg.com/bw/articles/2013-09-06/those-big-fat-chinese-weddings

Ning Hui, 'Born rich in China: explaining the disdain for "fu'erdai"', *Tea Leaf Nation*, http://www.tealeafnation.com/2013/03/born-rich-in-china-explaining-the-disdain-for-fuerdai/#sthash.as15U2OD.dpuf

Osnos, Evan, 'Angry youth: The new generation's neocon nationalists', *New Yorker*, http://www.newyorker.com/magazine/2008/07/28/angry-youth

Palmer, James, 'The balinghou', *Aeon*, http://aeon.co/magazine/society/james-palmer-chinese-youth/

Palmer, James, 'Kept women', *Aeon*, http://aeon.co/magazine/society/why-young-women-in-rural-china-become-the-mistresses-of-wealthy-older-men/

Schiavenza, Matt, 'Is gay marriage coming to China?', *The Atlantic*, http://www.theatlantic.com/china/archive/2013/06/is-gay-marriage-coming-to-china/277296/

Sebag-Montefiore, Clarissa, 'Meet the "lover-hunters" who help male Chinese millionaires find a wife', *The Telegraph*, http://www.telegraph.co.uk/women/womens-life/10383009/Meet-the-lover-hunters-who-help-male-Chinese-millionaires-find-a-wife.html

Tsai, Michelle, 'Everything you always wanted to know about sex (but didn't learn because you grew up in China)', *Slate*, http://www.slate.com/articles/news_and_politics/dispatches/2009/11/everything_you_always_wanted_to_know_about_sex_but_didnt_learn_because_you_grew_up_in_china.html

Zhai, Keith, '"Pick-up artist" Christopher Wu teaches Chinese men how to woo women', *South China Morning Post*, http://www.scmp.com/news/china/article/1292236/christopher-wu-teaches-chinese-men-how-woo-women

Zhang, Lijia, 'Sex abuse and China's children', *New York Times*, http://www.nytimes.com/2014/05/02/opinion/sex-abuse-and-chinas-children.html